Ratnakar Mahavihara
A Vajrayana Buddhist Monastery of Patan

Ratnakar Mahavihara
A Vajrayana Buddhist Monastery of Patan

Shanker Thapa
Indra Kumari Bajracharya

ADROIT
ADROIT PUBLISHERS
DELHI-110 002

Published by
ADROIT PUBLISHERS
4675/21, Ganpati Bhawan, Ansari Road,
Daryaganj, New Delhi-110 002
Phones : 011-23266030

Distributors
AKHIL BOOK DISTRIBUTORS
e-mail: akhilbooks@yahoo.com
akhilbooks@hotmail.com

ISBN : 81-87392-66-5

Layout
Sudhir Vatsa

Laser Typeset by
Arpit Printographers
E-mail : arpitprinto@yahoo.com

Printed in India on behalf of M/s Adroit Publishers
by Arpit Printographers
Phones : 09350809192, 011-22825424

CONTENTS

PREFACE

The study of Vihara culture in Newar Buddhism is very important in order to gain an understanding of Newar Buddhism. The role of the Vihara *Sangha* continues to be prominent in rites, rituals and other religious practices. All the Vajrayana Viharas are prototypes of each other.

Various researchers have showed a keen interest in the study of Vihara and studied using different conceptual paradigms and models, but very few researchers paid attention to the study of Ratnakara Mahavihara even though it occupies an important place in the history of Buddhism in Patan (Nepal). This Vihara was an educational center in ancient times. It is said that the famous Tibetan Guru Marpa had his *Dekha* initiation at this Vihara, where he lived for 3 years. This belief has made this Vihara even more important.

Different kinds of Buddhist rituals are performed in this Vihara throughout the year and it has several rituals that are unlike those of any other Vihara. This has made this Vihara unique in Patan. The living tradition of Kumari is one of the important features of this *baha*.

We regret that we could not access any of the written documents that were preserved by the *Ajus* in the Vihara. Not a single member of the *Sangha* gave us any kind of information during the research. We imagine that there must be *bahi Dhala Pau* records and other written documents in the possession of this Vihara, but in the name of secrecy, they are not accessible to anybody. Instead, we reconstructed the history of this Vihara from fragments of evidence. One should know that history is being destroyed in the name of secrecy.

The book is divided into nine chapters:

Chap. 1. This chapter contains the introduction, objectives, limitations and research methodology applied during the research. The introduction gives an overall picture of this book.

Chap. 2. This chapter discusses the conceptual aspects of *Viharas* in general and Nepalese *Viharas* in particular. It focuses on sub-themes such as the origin and historicity of the *Vihara* as well as various other aspects of ancient Nepalese *Viharas*. In this chapter, ancient inscriptions relating to the *Vihara* and the *Bhikshu* and *Bhikshuni Sangha* are described. It also discusses the functional role of the *Viharas*.

Chap. 3. In this chapter History of Buddhism in Nepal is dealt. In the beginning, it traces about Tibetan sources on Nepalese Buddhist history. Similarly, mythological tradition is also dealt to proceed to authentic history of Nepalese Buddhism. It is analysed on the basis of *Swayambhu Purana* and *Bhasa Vamshavali*. The historical context of *Swayambhu Chaitya* and visit of Emperor Ashoka are traced on the basis of classical texts. It further deals with Buddhist history during the *Lichhivi* and *Malla* periods analysing existing inscriptional sources. Finally, history of *Theravada* tradition of Nepal is also analysed to some extent.

Chap. 4. This chapter focuses on the general features and different kinds of modern day Nepalese *Viharas,* and describes various other *Viharas* in Patan.

Chap. 5. This chapter is devoted to *Hakha baha*, which is the main body of this work. This chapter discusses the heritage and significance of Ratnakar Mahavihara and describes various inscriptions, *Kacha baha*, *baha Sangha* and its organization.

Chap. 6. This chapter mainly focuses on the types of rituals and worship which are performed at *Hakha baha,* and describes several kinds of initiations such as *Barechoegu*, *Achaluyegu* and *Dekha*. It also describes *Guthis* such as *Sandepuja Guthi*, *Lainkebhu Guthi*, *Sana Guthi, Bicha Guthi* and other *Guthis* which operated in *Hakha baha*. The roles played by the *Sangha* members are also described in this book.

Chap. 7. *Hakha baha* has a distinct place among the *Viharas* of Patan due to the Institution of *Kumari*. This chapter deals with the tradition of *Kumari* at *Hakha baha* and mainly focuses on the selection procedures and cultural and ritual aspects related to *Kumari*. Alongwith this description, other *Viharas*' relationship with *Hakha baha* which relates to *Kumari* worship is also explained.

Chap. 8. The main focus of this chapter is the description of the structural features of *Hakha baha*. The architectural features, art forms, and images housed in *Hakha baha* are described in this chapter.

Chap. 9. This chapter concludes the book, and is followed by the glossary, appendix, bibliography and Index.

The research which we undertook was in fact a tough job for us, but many individuals inspired and helped us throughout. It would have been impossible to write this book without their help. We are particularly thankful to Mr. Milan Ratna Shakya for his help.

We are very much thankful to Mrs. Millicent Allysa Pugh (Thapa) who edited this manuscript. Her meticulous effort to go through with tiresome writings is really praiseworthy. Especially, we must thank her for editing skills and comments she made at appropriate places.

We are grateful to Min Bahadur Shakya, a visiting lecturer in the Department of Buddhist Studies, Tribhuvan University, Kirtipur. He kindly permitted us to use his library.

We would also like to say thanks to........ We cannot forget the help of Hera Kazi Vajracharya of *Bu Baha,* Patan, who provided us with some material during the research. His assistance proved to be very helpful in writing this book.

We are also thankful to Gajanan Dhakhwa, for taking some of the photos of Ratnakar Mahavihara (*Hakha baha*). We would also like to thank Hasana Shakya for typing a part of the manuscript.

Last but not the least, we must thank Ven. Prajnamurti of Anandakuti Vihara, a common friend of us and a student of Buddhism at Chulalongkorn Rajkiya Mahavidyalaya, University of Bangkok for his best wishes.

Shanker Thapa
Indra K. Bajracharya

1

INTRODUCTION

The term *Vihara* is called *baha* or *bahal* in Newari, but local people pronounce it *ba* instead of *baha*. In the Kathmandu Valley, many *Viharas* were established at different times. Since, Patan is predominantly a Buddhist city, it has many prominent *bahal* which were established by various individuals. At present, there are fifteen main *bahal* in Patan. Most of the *bahal* have *Kacha baha* and *Nani* affiliated with them and each *baha* has two names, one in Sanskrit and the other in Newari.

The *bahal* are the centers of religious activities, and played a role of immense significance in Buddhist cultural development. The *Sangha* of the followers exists in each *Vihara* within its boundary. In modern times, the major function of a Vajrayana *Vihara* in Nepal is only to perform elaborate rituals. Nepalese Buddhism has turned into a type of ritualized Buddhism rather than emphasizing philosophical values.

The *bahal* in Patan are prototype of one another; there are no major differences, however, minor variations may occur in Ratnakar Mahavihara, onc of fifteen main Viharas in Patan. Its Sanskrit name is *Shri Laksmi Kalyana Varma Samskarita Ratnakar Mahavihara*, but it is popularly known as *Hakha baha* or *Ha baha*. It was also called *Hatko baha*, and it is situated at ward no. 18, *Ga bahal*, in Patan.

Ratnakar Mahavihara is one of the most popular *bahals* of Patan.

It has preserved its typical Buddhist art and architecture as well as its ritual heritage. In this *Vihara*, there is the tradition of the living goddess, called *Kumari*. This practice is unique among the *Viharas* of Patan. Ratnakar Mahavihara *Sangha* has only Vajracharya members whereas other *Vihara Sanghas* in Patan have both Shakyas and Vajracharyas as members. The *Sangha* members become *Dyopala* at the shrine of *Kwapadyo* in turns, from the eldest to the youngest. A *Dyopala* is appointed only for the period of fifteen days. The *Sangha* has a committee of ten elders who are called *Aju*. One person is always in reserve, and acts as the *Ajus*' helper. The eldest *Aju* is called *Chakreshwar*. He plays an important role during the *Barechuyegu* (initiation) and *Achaluyegu* ceremonies. The *Ajus* meet once a month on the full moon day for tantric *puja* (*Agam puja*), and again on the tenth day of the dark half of each month for a ritual feast. This *Vihara* has *Sangha Bhojan Guthi* (*Sandey puja*), *Acharya Guthi*, *Sana Guthi* (death *Guthi*) and *Bicha Guthi.* Various other rituals are also observed at this *Vihara* from time to time.

Statement of the Problems

The study of *Viharas* is of immense significance in the study of Nepalese Buddhism. The *Viharas* of Kathmandu Valley in general and Patan in particular play a major role in the cultural and religious activities of the *Sangha*. The *Sangha* organization and its functions, rituals, art etc., are important components of a Vajrayana *Vihara*. If one intends to study the *Sangha*, the *Viharas* require a detailed study.

The *Ajus* also play a significant role in *Vihara* activities. They are the ones who are responsible for preserving Buddhism in its traditional form.

The tradition of the living goddess *Kumari* at *Hakha baha* is a significant feature of this *Vihara*, which has made this *Vihara* more prestigious than other *Viharas* in Patan. All of these factors have made *Hakha baha* in Patan important.

Vihara, as the source of cultural tradition and its continuity, requires a detailed analysis. As for the *Hakha baha*, empirical research is always lacking in the analysis of its role in society and culture.

Review of Literature

Viharas play an important role in Buddhist religion and culture, but researchers have not yet studied them properly. It is possible to study them from different perspectives, but there are only a few researchers who have written about this *Vihara*.

The book entitled *Buddhist Monasteries of Nepal* mainly deals with the monasteries of Kathmandu Valley. In this book, *Hakha baha* is also described briefly. The description mainly deals with the historical aspect of *baha* and some of its ritual activities, but lacks an indepth analysis.[1]

Another book, entitled *Ratnakar Mahavihara Ka Sankshipta Parichaya*, in Newari, describes the history of the *baha* art, architecture, *Guthi* and includes a list of the recipients of the *acharyabhisheka.* Although this book is informative, but it is not academic and is very brief. It does not even cover the main aspects of *Hakha baha*.[2]

The book *Yalaya Bauddha Vihara Sankhipta Parichaya* is mainly about the *Viharas* of Patan. It also deals with existing *Ajus*, *Kacha baha* and gives a brief history. It is in the form of a compiled book.[3]

History of Nepal is also about Buddhism in Nepal, and mentions that *Hakha baha* was torn down and was rebuilt at its present location by the order of King Siddhi Narsingha Malla, in order to extend the palace complex. No other facts are available regarding the topics in this book.[4] *The Cult of Kumari Virgin Worship in Nepal* also deals with the *Kumari* of the *Hakha baha*[5], which is also an important aspect of the *baha.*

H. A. Oldfield's book *Sketches from Nepal* also gives a brief introduction to *Hakha baha*.[6]

An article written on *Hakha baha* by Indra Kumari Bajracharya describes the history of *Hakha baha,* the structural characteristics of the *baha Sangha*, *Guthi*, *Kumari*, and so on.[7]

Aside from these works, no other separate work has yet been done on *Hakha baha*. The *baha* is mentioned in various contexts in independent studies. No other books and articles have been written so far. The present research is different to all these published works in terms of themes and the area of study.

Objectives

The general objective of this research is to analyse different aspects of *Hakha baha*. Some of the major objectives are as follows:

1. To analyse the conceptual aspects of Buddhist *Vihara*.
2. To make an assessment of general features of Nepalese Buddhist *Viharas*.
3. Critically analyse the historical aspect of *Hakha baha* using available inscriptions.
4. To make an assessment of rituals and worship organized in *Hakha baha*.
5. To describe the *Hakha baha Sangha*.
6. To examine the tradition of *Kumari* at *Hakha baha* and her role in Buddhist rituals in Patan.
7. To describe the structural characteristics and evaluate the art and architecture of *Hakha baha*.

Limitations of the Study

As the title suggests, this study is confined to Ratnakar Mahavihara (*Hakha baha*) of Patan. The historical aspect of the study is about its establishment, and was mainly based on the basis of historical evidence. However, the other aspects of the *Viharas* focus on current data, and most of the worship rituals, *Guthi, Kumari* etc. were studied based on present activities. The analysis are mainly descriptive.

Research Methodology

Both primary and secondary data are used in this book, and conclusion has been drawn based on these. Most of the information has been derived from primary sources, which comprised of historical documents such as metal, wood and stone inscriptions. Senior *Ajus* and other *Sangha* members of *Hakha baha* were interviewed, and the information they provided proved to be useful. During the interview the legends and stories related to this *baha* were also collected. All the research is based on an analysis of the cultural heritage of Ratnakar Mahavihara.

Observation is another important method that was used to collect information. The researcher observed various rituals and ceremonies that were performed in the *Vihara* during the research and collected relevant information. Secondary sources were also used in order to authenticate the description. Other sources include various published and unpublished thesis, related books, and journal articles. These sources support the interpretation and analysis of various themes.

Reference

1. John K. Locke: *Buddhist Monasteries of Nepal*, Kathmandu: Sahyogi Press, 1985, pp. 148-53.
2. Surya Man Vajracharya: *Ratnakara Mahavihara Ka Sankshipta Parichaya*, Patan: Dhusa Jyasha, B.S., 2050, pp.1-40.
3. Hera Kaji Vajracharya: *Yalaya Bauddha Vihara Sankshipta Parichaya*, Lalitpur: Bauddha Vihara Sangha, 2057, pp. 85-92.
4 Dainel Wright, *History of Nepal,* Translated from Parbatiya, Calcutta: Sushila Gupta, 1958 pp. 1-180.
5 Michael Allen: *The Cult of Kumari Virgin Worship in Nepal*, Kathmandu: Madhab Lal Mahajan, 1982, pp. 34-42.
6 Henry A. Oldfield: *Sketches from Nepal,* vol. II, Cosmo Publication, Delhi, 1974, pp. 1-356.
7. Indra Kumari Vajracharya: 'Nepalese Buddhist Monasteries: Aspects of Lakshmi Kalyana Varma 'Samskarita Ratnakar Mahavihara of Patan', *Voice of History*, Vol. XV, No. 2. Kirtipur: B.S., 2057, pp. 69-82.

2

THE RISE OF THE VIHARA IN BUDDHISM

Buddhism and Brahmanic Tradition

The ultimate goal of practicing all kinds of religions is to attain enlightenment, cultivate wisdom, attain eternal bliss or deserve a rightful place in one of the heavenly spheres. The ancient *Brahmanas* believed that all the paths lead to union with *Brahma*, the highest God. According to Buddhism, *Brahmaloka*, the highest sphere of existence, is attained through the practice of four *Brahma vihara* (*Maitri*, *Karuna*, *Mudita* and *Upekshya*), but union with *Brahma*, according to the *Brahmana* texts, was possible only through the study of the Vedas or performance of sacrifice. Buddhism preferred to renounce the worldly desires and lead an austere life of a *Brahmachari* (celibate) and practice the four *Brahmaviharas* to attain the ultimate truth.[1]

Motivated by holy goals of life, different types of asceticism were practiced which were largely governed by the customary laws. The ascetic practice has been the governing factor of religious life among the *Paribrajakas* in ancient India. The practice of wandering mendicancy had been existing long before Gautama introduced his philosophical tradition. The ancient *Paribrajakas* lived outside the society. They were the community of homeless who survived on begging alms. So, they moved from one place to another except in the rainy season. Among the ancient *Paribrajaka*, the *Sramanas* deserved highly respectable status and a distinguished place in the society. During the 6th century B.C., they were highly respected among the wandering mendicants. Thus, the history of wandering mendicancy and ascetic practices go back to remote antiquity. The practice of such type of asceticism was very popular. So, the *Paribrajaka* community formed a populous and influential group of people of the same kind. Of course, they had their own customs, usages, manners, ideas and practices. The Buddhist *Sangha* differed from other wandering sects and also became distinct among the contemporary wandering ascetics. The practice of rain retreats in ancient times was common among the *Paribrajakas* belonging to different sects. The practice of rain retreat took shape of permanent sanctuary institution during the course of history. The Buddhist *Sangha* signified the cenobite society of residents at the *Avasa*.[2]

The term asceticism, for the ancient *Paribrajakas*, denoted to the total denial of any kind of desire (*Kama*) intending attainment of spiritual goal. Hence, the ascetics essentially require refraining from *Kama* (desire), *Krodha* (anger), *Lobha* (greed) and *Moha* (illusion). Human society has followed asceticism since the remote antiquity. The ascetic practices were observed due to various reasons. In fact, the fear from demons, the view that one must be in a ritual purity as a necessary condition for entering into communion with the supernatural, desire to invite the divine beings, idea of earning piety, compassion and salvation, the sense of sin and guilt that prompt need for atonement, the power of dualistic concepts that have been at the source of efforts to free the spiritual part of men from defilement of the body, etc. led to renounce the world and enter the *Paribrajaka* community.[3] Three types of asceticism- ritual, disciplinary and mystical—were practiced. Such practices aimed at training the soul. The *Yoga* in Hinduism, the *eight-fold path* in Buddhism[4] and *spiritual exercises* in Christianity are varied types of asceticism. It has been a recognized opinion during Buddha's lifetime that a deeper insight into the meaning of life could be obtained through practicing severe asceticism which would free the soul from physical bondage. During Buddha's lifetime, a number of ascetic groups were in existent who, leaving the worldly society, followed the way of homelessness. They were popularly known as the *Parivrajaka, Bhikshu, Sramana, Yatin, Sanyasin* etc. They practiced asceticism under the *Gurus* (the teachers) according to their teachings.[5] The *Suttanipata* mentions that ancient sages were ascetics who lived in self-control of sense. Of course, they lived on food donated by the followers. They lived as the *Brahmacharin* in the quest of knowledge and good conduct. They held austerities, rectitude, tenderness, love and forbearance in high esteem.[6] The ultimate goal of the *Brahmanas* during the 6th century B.C. was to attain *Brahma* by acquisition of merit through austere practices. The *Brahmanic* tradition in the 5th century B.C. combined asceticism with animal sacrifice. Those extreme forms of asceticism were limited within the *Jain, Ajivika* and other non-*Brahmanic* sects.[7] In the ancient times, asceticism was practiced only when it was necessary for proper performances. The contemporary society believed that one could purge of effects of former deeds by ascetic practices. The *Parivrajaka* who practiced asceticism, were homeless wanderers. They renounced the worldly society for religious motives. Many of them hailed from the *Brahmin* society. References are found in the *Samyaka Nikaya* and *Suttanipata* that women also led the life of a *Parivrajika* (female wanderers).[8]

Early Buddhists did not regard Buddha different from other visionaries and ascetics except that he was the discoverer and the teacher of the path.[9] The practical rules were not framed on ascetic basis because strenuous efforts of bodily and sensual faculties had no intrinsic value for *Buddha*. Buddha rejected the prevailing system of asceticism although instances are found that some Buddhist practitioners practiced asceticism to reach the religious goal.

Various forms of asceticism have been sanctioned in the world religions. The ascetic practices were observed through celibacy, denial of material goods, abstinence, fasting, bodily mortification and so on.[10] Physically, exhausting exercises as a form of asceticism is still very much common among the Hindu ascetics in India. It has centuries long history. Syrian Christianity and other tribal religions also practice bodily mortification as part of asceticism. The later Vedic period encouraged ascetic use of *Tapa* (austerity), which was inspired by the belief that it emancipates all kinds of sins. Lateron, the practice was embedded into *Brahmanism* too. Even ascetic practice has been promoted in the basic teachings of Buddha. The fact that *Dukha* (suffering) lies in casual relation with *Kama* (desire) connotes the importance of asceticism although Buddha was against ascetic practices. Buddha also once became an ascetic alms man. The practice of asceticism was already in existence in ancient India before his advent. The *Upanishads* (religious philosophical treatises) with emphasis on *Tyaga* (renouncement) as the supreme virtue are the philosophical sources of Hindu ascetic movements in the early stage.[11] The ritual of *Prabajjya* (going forth) is viewed as the basis of institutionalization of asceticism in Buddhism.[12] It entailed rejection of the whole system of Vedic social practice. It is, therefore, called *Sanyasa* (the complete casting off).[13] They called *Prabajjya—agarasma angarima* (from home to homeless). The wandering ascetics within the Buddhist *Bhikshus* or the *Paribrajaka* community originated the *Sangha* order. All kinds of Hindu or Buddhist asceticism intend to conquer the worldly desires. The Buddhist monastic order represents the middle way between material indulgence and bodily mortification. It avoided both the extremes practiced by other non-Buddhists of the day. Thus, the physical austerities and bodily mortification were restricted in the Buddhist monastic order. Buddhists believe that bodily mortification does not help to achieve ostensible goal and extinction of desire either sexual or material.[14]

Hindu social organization prefers the *Varna* system (the four type or the caste hierarchy) and four *Ashramas* (the stages of life). The *Ashrama* is closely connected with the ascetic mode of life.[15] Its history goes back to the *Upanishad* era. The *Brahadaranayka* and *Chhandogya Upanishad* deal with various stages of *Ashrama*. However, Buddha believed that life of a householder is superior to all other stages of life.[16] During Buddha's life time, the Buddhist community revolted against the contemporary society. Most probably, the Buddhist monastic order has modified rules and declared that one could renounce if he considers himself fit for that. Buddha and his followers considered only one stage of life against widely accepted four stages of life in the *Vedic* tradition.

The monastic rules in Buddhism differ to other wandering *Parivrajakas.* Various rules were framed to prepare entrants able to correspond with the Buddhist ideal of monastic life. Thus Ten Commandments (*Shikshapadas)* were created.[17]

The lay believers also secured significant place in the Buddhist mode of life and religious practices. They offered alms and fulfilled other material needs of the Buddhist monks. So, they had no worries about subsistence needs, and it made them able to devote full-time in the pursuit of spiritual quest. This was very much common even among the other *Brahmanic* or *non-Brahmanic* wandering mendicants. Thus, the lay believers played a significant role in the development of wandering mendicancy and ascetic practices. The lay believers did not make any distinction between Buddhist and non-*Buddhist* ascetics. No distinction was made while donating alms. So, donation of alms to the Buddhist monks did not necessarily mean that the *Upasakas* had given up the faith and ignored *Brahmanic* values. The *Brahmans*, who spoke to Buddha and became his *Upasaka*, did not necessarily change social and ritual systems thereby. They remained always *Brahmins*.[18] The laity could maintain familial duties, and perform customary rites provided they did not offend the obligatory rules of *Ahimsa* (non-violence). It was obligatory for them to take refuge in the Three Jewels (*Tri-Ratna*), believe in five moral vows and listen preaching on the *Uposatha* days, during which eight moral vows were observed.[19] The *Upasakas* were permitted to enter the monastic order or leave the community of monks if they so desired. The *Ashrama* system in Hinduism was a permanent institution. Buddhism also marked gradual changes in its philosophical tradition. The *Mahayanists* developed *Saddharmapundarika Sutra* (the Lotus of the Good Law), *Gandavyuha Sutra* and *Mahayana Sutra* as the basis of the philosophical tradition.[20] They believe that ultimate salvation is due to the worship, prayer, etc. of the Buddha and other Buddhist cults. The worship of deities and practicing meditation aim at realization of the ultimate truth. In many Buddhist countries like Nepal, India,

Sri Lanka, Myanmar, China, Thailand, Korea and Japan, Buddha is worshipped as an incarnation. In the Tibetan *Mahayana,* Dalai Lama (Tib: *Talai bLama*), the head of the *Yellow Hats* or the *dGelugs pa* sect, has been recognized as the incarnation of the Bodhisattva of Compassion—*Avalokiteswar* (Tib: *Chenrezi*, Kor: *Kwan-Se-Um-Bosal*, Ch: *Kwan-Yin* and Jap.: *Kannon*). The Hindus, in the mythologies of *Mahabharata, Ramayana* and *Purana* also believed in incarnation. They also believe *Buddha* as one of the ten incarnations of *Lord Vishnu*, the Hindu God of protection. The *Varaha Purana*, *Agni Purana* and some other later *Puranas* recognize incarnation.

Buddhist treatises such as the *Dhammapada* and the *Vinayapitaka* do not sanction the acts of worship. The evolution of atheistic Buddhism into theistic *Mahayana* was due to the religious fervour of its *Upasaka* and *Upasika*, and the *Bhikshus* under dominating influence of Hindu theism. The Hindu doctrine of dedication of action to the God as taught in *Gita* (the songs of God), supplies an obvious parallelism to the belief of *Mahayana* in *Bodhisattva* ideal. Bodhisattva is one who postpones self-enlightenment for the benefit of the sentient beings and destined to be enlightened.[21]

Being a theistic religion, Hinduism believes in the existence of various Gods—the highest self of singular *Brahmana* (the absolute essence of the all) and the *Jivatman* (the individual soul). Certain types of similarities in the practical aspects of Buddhism and Hinduism made it difficult to understand Buddhism without prior knowledge of *Vedic* lore and *Upanishadic* doctrines.[22] The culture-religious tradition prevailed in India during Buddha's life time was completely based on *Vedic* and *Upanishadic* philosophy. It lays emphasis on *Jnana* (knowledge) than on *Karmic* activities. This powerful force of the *Karma* of a man is the main factor in rebirth. Hence, Buddhism lays emphasis on the eight-fold path.

Buddhism borrowed many of the philosophical tenets from the *Yoga* and *Samkhya* philosophies. There is the common view on suffering *(dukhavada)* and the doctrine of Transmigration (*Janmantaravada).*[23] *Mahayana* movement was greatly influenced by the revival of the *Brahmanical* faiths during the 2nd to the 5th century A.D., although it was stronger in volume and material. The monastic rules of the *Pratimoksha* were first adopted from the *Brahmanical* codes. The observance of celibacy and five precepts of good conduct resemble the same tradition.[24] Those rules were rearranged to provide normative principle for the Buddhist monastic order.[25]

The Buddhist monasticism is similar to that of Hindu *Sanyasa* system in which an aspirant renounces the world and isolates himself from the rest of the society. Thus, a *Sanyasi* remains outside the social boundary. So, he is a person living outside the existing social structure, and his quest, in the Indian context, is an extreme state of an individual pursuing his own salvation.[26] This type of *Brahmanical* asceticism was a model for the early Buddhist practitioners. The ancient *Parivrajaka* gave rise to all types of wandering mendicancy. The ancient concepts of *Nirganthi* and *Vairagi* were equally applicable to the Buddhist ascetic practice which mean—without ties and free from affection (*Nirganthi*—without knots; and *Vairagi*-religious recluse). During the course of time, they created indigenous traditions and systems of contemplation and organization.

The monastic tradition is very old in world religions. The traces of monastic practice are also found in Egypt, Palestine and Syria. In India, eremite life was the earliest form of monasticism. The rigorous ascetic practices were in vogue in the pre-Buddhist times attaining its climax in the 6th century B.C.[27] Monasticism adopted by the Buddhists was quite unknown in India. It was a different type of system which differed to the prevailing ascetic practices adopted by the *Brahmanic* or non-*Brahmanic* groups. They also lived a communal life, but they lacked a definite code of conduct. The traditional usages and the leaders governed the community. Only the *Jaina* monastics developed such a code. The Buddhists have their own rules or code called the *Pratimoksha* or the V*inayapitaka*. They laid emphasis on mental discipline rather than physical. So, even in the ancient times, the Buddhists were not required to go unnecessary physical discomfort. The necessary things to practice concentration were—a little food and cloth, a bare bed and seat, medicaments and a resting place. Before the development of permanent monastic settings, *Bhikshus* lived in forests and caves. The minimum requisites (*Nissayas*) prescribed for them are as follows[28]—

- To take food only received as alms (*Pindiyalopa bhojanam*)
- Use robes made out of rags collected from dust heaps. (*Pansukulasenasanam*)
- To sit and lie at the foot of a tree. (*Rukhamulasenasanam*)
- To use excrement and cow's urine as medicines (*Putimuttabaesajam*)

In addition to this, the early *Bhikshus* were also required to follow fourteen *Dhutangas* (precepts of ascetic practices) which are mentioned in the V*isuddhimagga*. The *Dhutangas* include—wearing robes, begging alms for food, begging house to house without omission, to eat at one sitting, to keep only one bowl, not to take any food after finishing meal, dwell only in forests not at the outskirts of towns and villages, to live in places without shed and under a tree, to live in an open place, to use whatever bed or seats allotted and to spend nights by sitting not by lying.[29]

If a *Bhikshu* practiced severe *Dhutanga*; he did not require practicing the less severe *Dhutanga*. So, it did not matter as to how many *Dhutangas* a monk practiced. For nuns eight *Dhutangas* were binding. At the same time, the lay believers were required to observe only two of them.

Dhutangas were elaborated from the minimum requisites of the *Nissayas*. The observance of *Dhutangas*, in fact, represented a kind of limit of permissible asceticism.

Conceptual Aspect of Vihara

The term *Vihara* comes from Sanskrit word *Viharati*, which means to walk or to sit, thus to walk peacefully.[30] In fact, *Viharas* were originally built to accommodate monks and nuns and facilitate their religious practices. Therefore, a *Vihara* is a secluded place where the members of the *Sangha*, those who renounce worldly desires, live together and practice the *Dharma*. The monks travelled according to season. It is said that they wandered like rhinoceros.[31] The three month long rainy season made it miserable for them to wander for alms, so the monks were expected to reside at one place and devote themselves to their religious practice during the monsoon.[32] The places set up for rain retreats (*Vassavasa*) were situated near villages. It is also assumed that the practitioners probably built huts and gathered fortnightly to recite *pratimoksha* (Pali: *patimokha*) rules. Gautam Buddha also permitted his followers to live in abodes such as *Vihara*, *Addhyaoga* (pinnacle house) *Prasada* (big buildings), *Hommiya* (an attic), *Guha* (caves) and under trees.[33] The concept of *Viharas* was developed accordingly. Four types of *Guha* are mentioned in the *Vinaya* text—brick *Guhas*, stone *Guhas*, wood *Guhas*, and soil *Guhas*.[34] The practice of *Vassavasa* (or rain retreats), was common for all in ancient India. Later, during Buddha's lifetime, donors dedicated various *Viharas* to the Buddhist *Sangha*. The lavish donations made by King Bimbsara and Anathapindaka are mentioned in the Pali canons.[35]

Thus, a *Vihara* is a Buddhist monastery, a place where Buddhist monks or nuns live together for religious pursuit. Buddhist canonical literature uses the terms *Arama* and *Vihara* to denote dwelling places for monks. In the beginning, a living place that was to be used by the Buddha was called an *Arama*. During Gautam Buddha's lifetime, Benuvana in Rajgriha was called an *Arama*.[36] The residential complex constructed for Buddha and his disciples by Anathapindaka was called *Vihara*. This fact shows that Gautam Buddha and his disciples started to live in *Aramas* and *Viharas* in the beginning. This is also described in ancient Buddhist literature such as *Avadana* and *Jataka* stories. The famous *Aramas* are *Jetavanarama*, *Nigrodharama*, *Ghositarama* and *Purbarama*. All these are mentioned as famous dwelling places of Buddha and his disciples. In one *Arama*, there were many *Viharas*, so, the *Vihara* itself used to be a part of the *Arama*. A group of *Viharas* came to be called *Arama*.[37] The frame narratives in Pali cannons state:

> *Avam me Suta Eka Samaya Bhagawan Sawathiya Viharati*
> *Jetavaney Anathapindakasya Aramey...*

(Thus I heard, once the Lord stayed in the Anathapindakarama at Jetavan......)

It emphasizes that *Vihara* were existent in ancient India during Buddha's lifetime.[38] In fact, *Viharas* were built to protect the monastics from rain and accommodate them to continue practice during the rainy season.[39] *Viharas* were built of brick in Varanasi and Kapilvastu in the 3rd century B.C. Most of the *Viharas* in India were built from 5th to 12th centuries including Nalanda, Vikramshila, Vallabhi, Jagaddala and Odantapuri, which were very famous Buddhist institutions in ancient India.[40] The transformation of residences into centers of learning is indeed remarkable in the history of Buddhism in India.[41] After the 5th century, most *Viharas* were built on plains in India. This has been proved by archaeological surveys of the Taxila, Sarnath, Nalanda and Vikramshila Mahaviharas.[42] A Gupta period clay bowl found in Kumharar in India mentions the *Arogya Vihara Bikhu Sanghasaya*.[43] Lichhivi inscriptions also make reference to the *Arya Bhikshu Sangha* and *Arya Bhikshuni Sangha*. The phrase in the clay pot inscription refers to a living place for monks, which is called *Vihara*. According to one reference in the Buddhist literature, a *Shresthi* or merchant, built sixty *Viharas* in Rajgriha for Buddhist monks.[44] Monasteries, since ancient times, have symbolized Buddhism and have been a symbol of strength which reflect the thoughts, culture, aspirations and intellectual development of the people.[45]

Nepalese Vihara in Ancient Times

No archaeological evidence has been found so far in the Kathmandu Valley, which gives information about the origin of the *Viharas* in Nepal. According to Wright's geneology, the *Gopala* dynasty ruled Kathmandu Valley for 521 years and *Mahipala* dynasty ruled for 161 years.[46] Buddhism wasn't practiced during those periods, and no evidence contradicts this hypothesis. Therefore, the *Gopala* and *Mahipala* dynasties are referred to as pre-Buddhist periods. After these periods, the *Kirata* dynasty ruled in Nepal. This period was important in terms of the origin and development of Buddhism in Nepal. In the Kathmandu Valley, many inscriptions, colophons, coins and manuscripts relating to Buddhism have been found. Historians claim that Buddhism first came to Nepal during the *Kirata* period. Wright's geneology mentions that Shakyamuni Buddha came to Nepal (Valley of Kathmandu) from Kapilvastu during the reign of seventh *Kirata* King Jitedasti (465 B.C.), in order to visit *Swayambhu*, *Manjushri puchhagra*, *Guhyeswari* and *Namobuddha* mountain.[47] In *Mulasarvastivada Vinaya*, it is mentioned that Ananda, one of Buddha's disciples, came to Nepal to meet the Shakyas of Kapilvastu who used to live in Nepal in order to escape the atrocities of Viruddhaka. According to this account, his feet were frostbitten during his return from Nepal. For this reason, Buddha gave the *Bhikshus* permission to wear shoes.[48] From this, it may be assumed that *Bhikshu* Ananda and the Shakyas introduced Buddhism to ancient Nepal. But historical evidence to support this hypothesis is still lacking.

The *Vamsavali* states that Mauryan Emperor Ashoka came to Nepal during the time of Kirata King Sthunko and built many monasteries and Chaityas. He also founded a new town and built four stupas. Those Chaityas are Tetathura, Puchothura, Ebithura, Laganthura, located on each corner of the town. The name of the town is called Ashoka Pattan. It is generally assumed that these four *Stupas* represent four epochs or ages—*Satyayuga*, *Tretayuga*, *Dvaparyuga* and *Kaliyuga*. *Vamsavali* also states that Ashoka's daughter Charumati married a local *Kshetriya* prince named Devapala and built a *Vihara* named Charumati *Vihara* in Chabahil (Maiju Bahal).[49] This, however, has not yet been proved. An inscription at Chabahil mentions the *Kinnari Jataka*, but there is no date on the inscription. This *bahil* attracted Chinese pilgrims and other Buddhist monks for several centuries. According to H. C. Kern, some of the oldest *Viharas* in the Kathmandu Valley are *Vikramshila Vihara* (*Tham Bahi* of Thamel), *Vishanukhya Vihara*, *Sri Chakra Vihara*, *Hemvarna Vihara* and *Bhuyu Bahal*, *Tri-Ratna Vihara* and *Bisnuchhyen Vihara*. These are first century *Viharas* of Kathmandu Valley.

Huien-T-sang, a Chinese traveller of the seventh century,

recorded 1000 *Viharas* in Kapilvastu,[50] which proves that the construction of *Viharas* was very popular in those days. The excavation of Kapilvastu also unearthed some important *Viharas* that existed during Buddha's time.[51] Mythological accounts of Buddhism aside, historically there has been evidence of Buddhism ever since ancient times.[52] The Lichhivi period was very favourable for Buddhists. Many rulers of that period patronized Buddhism and donated lavishly to construct and operate monasteries.

The names of various *Viharas* are found in Lichhivi inscriptions.[53] In this period, there were well-developed *Viharas*, which the Lichhivi kings established for religious purposes and protected. The *Hadigaon* inscription of Amshuvarma, dated *Samvat* 32 *Ashad*, states:

> *...Gum Viharasya pu6 pa2 Shri Man Viharasya pu6 pa2, Sr Ra (ja) Viharasya pu6 pa2 Khayurikanharasya pu6 pa2 Ma (dhya)maviharasya pu6 pa2 samanya Viharasya pu3 pa1...*

(6 *Purana* two *Pana* each was given to *Gum Vihara*, *Shree Man Vihara*, *Shree Raj Vihara*, *Kharjurika Vihara* and *Madhyama Vihara* and 3 *Purana* 8 *Pana* to all other ordinary *Viharas*)

The *Gopalrajvamsavali* also makes reference to the Buddhist *Viharas* of Kathmandu Valley.[54] During the Lichhivi period, there were both the *Bhikshu* and *Bhikshuni Sanghas*. The Hadigaon inscription mentioned *Gum Vihara, Man Vihara, Raj Vihara, Kharjurika Vihara, Madhyama Vihara and Samanya Vihara*. Similarly, Narendra Deva's Pashupati inscription referred to *Shiva Deva Vihara, Kharjurika Vihara*, and *Yangu baha*, Narendra Deva's inscription referred to *Shiva Deva, Mana Deva, Kharjurika, Madhyama, Abhayaruchi* and *Kalyanagupta Vihara*, and the Naxal inscription (Jaya Deva II) referred to—*Ajika Vihara* and Jiva *Varma Vihara*.[55]

Dhanavajra Vajracharya mentions the names of twenty *Viharas* in his *Licchavi Abhilekh*.[56] He also referred to some other *Viharas* that are referred to in the Lichhivi inscriptions, which include *Abhayaruchi Vihara*, *Vartakalyana Gupta Vihara* and *Chaturbhalasan Vihara*. These *Viharas* are mentioned in the

Yagabahal inscription of King Narendra Deva. *Shiva Deva Vihara* is another important *Vihara* which is mentioned in Pashupati's *Vajraghar* inscription,[57] and the *Arya Bhikshu Sangha* is also mentioned in the Vajraghar inscription. The Yagabahal inscription (*Samvat* 103) contains the words *Arya Bhikshu Sangha*, and the Vajraghar inscription mentions the *Chaturdisa* Arya *Bhikshu Sangha* (*Bhiskhu Sangha* of the four directions).[58] The inscription at Patan Chapata tole refers to the *Arya Bhikshuni Sangha*, and one of the inscriptions in Musumbahal mentions *Bhikshuni Sangha Samarpita pana purana*. Thus, on the basis of these inscriptions and other sources, we can conclude that many monasteries were constructed during the Lichhivi period. The Pashupati inscription of Jaya Deva II, dated *Samvat* 157, referred to King Vrisha Deva as *Sugat Sahsana Paksyapati* (He who favoured the rule of the Buddha). He constructed *Singu Vihara* Chaitya.[59] Others, including *Shiva Deva Vihara*, *Ajika Vihara*, *Abhayaruchi Vihara, Chaturtingkhasana Vihara, Mahaprati Vihara, Sujatprabhu Vihara, Vartakalyan Gupta Vihara, Pranidhi Vihara* and *Jawatma Vihara*, are the second type of eight Lichhivi *Viharas*.[60] Dharmaswami, a renowned Tibetan Buddhist scholar, came to Nepal from 1226 A.D to 1234 A.D. He mentioned some *Viharas*, such as *Swayambhu Vihara, Tham Vihara, Bhukham or Bungamati Vihara, Dhunta Vihara, Laliwan Vihara, Yampi Vihara, Kunti Vihara*, and *Pinta Vihara*, which existed during his stay in the Kathmandu Valley.[61] This proves that there were famous Buddhist centers in Nepal during the Lichhivi and Malla periods.

Since ancient times, the *Viharas* served the religious interests of the people. The Lichhivi period witnessed a steady growth in Buddhism. However, nothing is known about Buddhism from the 9th to the 12th centuries. This is considered to be a dark age in its history, but it is known that the *Viharas* continued to play the same role as they did in ancient times. The colophons of Buddhist manuscript that were written during this period also prove this fact.

Vihara were Buddhist religious centers in medieval times, when *Mahayana* Buddhism was predominant in the Kathmandu Valley. The Mahasanghika and Vajrayana came to Nepal in the ancient times,[62] and most of the *Viharas* then were established in the Patan area. The Ashtasahasarika Mahaprajnaparmita, which was written in N.S 128 and N.S 935, mentioned *Lhan Vihara.*[63] Similarly, another version of Ashtasahasarika Mahaprajnaparamita, dated N.S 235, referred to *Dharma Chakra Mahavihara* and *Pancharakshya* manuscript dated N.S. 434 mentions the *Karanda Vihara.*[64] Likewise a *dharani* manuscript dated N.S. 898 made reference to *Ta baha* of Patan.[65] Most of the existing *Viharas* in Nepal, in fact, are of medieval origin. Originally, walls surrounded them.[66] These *Viharas* served the same purpose as the early period *Viharas*, but their architecture changed in its form and style. The *Viharas* that exist now must have been renovated several times in later period, thereby bringing about changes in their medieval shape and features. These *Viharas* include *Paravata Mahavihara, Hiranyavarna Mahavihara, Rudravarna Mahavihara* and *Vikramashila Mahavihara.*

Buddhist *Viharas* in this period played an important role in educating people and teaching Buddhism. At that time, many scholars from India, China and Tibet came to Nepal for academic pursuits and stayed in various *Viharas*. Santarakshita, Atisa, Naropa, Marpa, Kamalasila and other scholars came to study Buddhism at different times. It is said that Marpa, the great translator of Tibet, stayed at *Ratnakar Vihara* for three years in order to study *Anuttarayoga tantra* under Paindapa and Chitherpa in the 11th century.[67]

Buddhism underwent several changes during the time of Jayasthiti Malla. His reforms brought about major changes in the Newar Buddhist social structure. Buddhist *Bhikshus*, for example, gave up celibacy and started to live with their families, but they were called *Brahmacharya Bhikshus*. The Vajracharyas, who were originally the most knowledgeable ones, merely became a group of priests, and made no efforts to increase the level of Buddhist scholarship. Consequently, there was a gradual decline in Buddhist society and Buddhist scholarship. The higher forms of tantric practice were not popular among them.

References

1. Nalinaksha Dutt: *Early Monastic Buddhism,* Calcutta: J.C. Sarkhel, 1941, pp. 14-17.
2. Sukumar Dutt: *Early Buddhist Monarchism*, London: Kegan Paul, 1924, pp. 17-19.
3. *The New Encyclopaedia Britannica*, Vol. II, Chicago: Helen Hemingway Bentom, 1979, p. 135.
4. The Eightfold path in Buddhism is a guideline to moral living. It is mentioned in the *Dirgha Nikaya*, *Sutra* 22 which includes right belief, right resolve, right speech, right action, right behaviour, right occupation and right concentration. H. Hackamann: *Buddhism As A Religion*, Delhi: Neeraj Publication, 1981, pp. 18-19; H.C. Warren: *Buddhism in Translations*, New York: Atheneum, 1963, p. 373.
5. G.S.P. Mishra: *The Age of Vinaya*, New Delhi: Munsiram Manohar Lall, 1972, p. 105.
6. Dutt: f. n. no. 1, pp. 8-10.
7. *Ibid*, p. 14.
8. *Samyutta Nikaya* III, and *Sutta Nipata* II, cited from: Dutt, f. n. no. 1, p. 33.
9. Joseph M. Kitagawa: *Religions of the East*, Philadelphia: West Minster, n.d., p. 175.
10. *The New Encyclopaedia* . . . , f. n. no. 3, pp. 135-36.
11. For further details on asceticism in India, see: Margaret Sinclair Stevenson, *The Heart of Jainism*, London: Oxford University Press, 1915, p. 2.
12. Melford E. Spiro: *Buddhism and Society: A Great Tradition and Its Burmese Viccissitudes*, Berkeley: University of California Press, 1982, p. 281.
13. Sukumar Dutt: *Buddhist Monks and Monasteries in India*, London: George Allen and Unwin, 1962, p. 41.
14. Spiro: f. n. no .12, p. 296.
15. The four *Ashramas* described in the *Upanishadic* tradition are: *Brahmacharya* (Celibacy or Chastity), *Grihastha* (Family life), *Vanaprastha* (Life in forest as recluse) and *Sanyasa* (Complete casting of).
16. N. Aiwaswamy Shastri: *'Approach To Hinduism'* in P.V. Bapat (ed.), *2500 Years of Buddhism*, New Delhi: Ministry of Information and Broadcasting, 1959, p. 345.
17. Mishra: f. n. no. 5, pp.117-18. The Ten Commandments mentioned

in the *Mahavagga* of the *Vinayapitaka* include to refrain from: taking life, taking what is not given, sexual activities, speaking lie, taking intoxicants, taking foods at wrong times, indulging in dance, songs etc., sleeping on high beds, decorating the body, and receiving silver or gold.

18. H. Oldenberg: *The Buddha*, W. Hoey (tr.), London: 1904, pp. 282-283.
19. Mahavagga Uposatha Skandhaka', Rahul Sankrityayan, *Vinayapitaka*, Varanasi: Mahabodhi Sabha, 1935, pp. 138-70.
20. Shastri: f. n. no. 16, p. 348; Also see: H. Kern, (Eng. tr.), 'Saddharmapundarika Sutra or the 'Lotus of The True Law' in F. Maxmuller (ed.), *The Sacred Books of The East*, Vol. 21, New Delhi: Motilal Benarsi Dass, 1925, pp. I-XXXVI.
21. *The Bhagvad Gita* is the song of God which is one of the important Hindu sacred scriptures.
22. This view was expressed by prominent Indian scholar Swami Vivekananda. Radha Govinda Basak, *Lectures on Buddha and Buddhism*, Calcutta: Sambodhi Publications, 1961, pp. 103-104.
23. *Ibid*, pp. 108-109.
24. E. J. Thomas: *The History of Buddhist Thought*, New York: Barnes and Noble, 1951, p. 1.
25. Kitagawa: f. n. no. 9, p. 173.
26. S. J. Tambiah: *Buddhism and The Spirit Cult In North East Thailand*, Cambridge: Cambridge University Press, 1970, p. 63.
27. Dutt: f. n. no. 1, p. 31.
28. Nalinaksha Dutt: *Early Monastic Buddhism*, Calcutta: K. L. Mukhopadhyaya, 1971, pp. 153-55.
29. Bhikshu Samyak S. Pranaputra: (tr. In Nepali), *Vishuddhimarga*, Kathmandu: Sukhihotu Nepal, 2058 B.S., pp. 54-74; Dutt, f. n. no. 28, pp. 156-58.
30. Bhikshu Sudarshan: *Nepali Vihara Ka Bishestaharu,* Lalitpur: Sradaluharu 2040 B.S., p. 1; *Also see*: Milan Shakya, *'Nepal ma Vihara Ko Prachin Parampara'*, *Paleswan*, Vol. IV, Lalitpur: Lotus Research Center, 1997, p. 27.
31. Sukumar Dutt: *Early Buddhist Monachism,* London: Kegan Paul, 1924, pp- 112-13.
32. *The Seeker's Glossary of Buddhism*, New York: Sutra Translation Committee of U.S.A and Canada, 1998, p. 508.
33. T.W Rhys Davis and H. Oldenberg: (tr.), *Vinaya Text* III, compiled in Maxmuller (ed.), *The Sacred Book of the East,* Vol. XX, New

Delhi: Motilal Banarasi Das, 1975, p. 175; *Also see*: Rahul Sankrityayan, *Vinayapitaka*, Taiwan: The Corporate Body of the Buddha Education Foundation, n.d, pp. 446-47.

34. *Ibid*.
35. Narada Thera: *The Buddha and His Teachings*, Malaysia: Buddhist Missionary Society, 1988, p. 166.
36. Basudeva Upadhyaya, *Prachin Bhartiya Stupa*, Patna: Hindi Grantha Academy, 1972, p. 7.
37. Bhikshu Sudarshan: f. n. no 30, p. 2.
28. *Ibid.*
39. Upadhyaya: f..n. no. 36, p. 98, *Also see*: Rajana Vajracharya, *Role of the Hiranayavarna Mahavihara in Socio-Cultural Life of the Buddhist Newarks* (Ph.D. Dissertation submitted to the Faculty of Humanities and Social Science, Tribhuvan University, Kathmandu: 2050 B.S, p. 60.
40. Crystal Mirror: *Light Of Liberation: A History Of Buddhism In India* Vol. VII, Berkeley: Dharma Publishing House, 1992, pp. 302, 334-35, 354, 361-62, 373-74, and 375-78.
41. Anukul Chandra Bannerjee: *Aspects of Buddhist Culture from Tibetan Sources*, Calcutta: K. L. Mukhopadhyaya, 1984, p. 80.
42. *Ibid*, *Also see*: Shakya, f. n. no. 30, p.29.
43. Shakya, f. n. no. 30, p.29; Vajracharya, f. n. no. 39, p. 60.
44. *Mahavagga* 1-4-17; *Also See: Shakya,* f. n. no 30, p. 29.
45. Bannerjee: f. n. no. 41, p. 80.
46. This geneology is not considered to be an authentic source.
47. Daniel Wright: *History of Nepal,* Translated from Parbatia, Calcutta: Sushil Gupta, 1958, pp 47-65; Hemraj Shakya: *Swayambhu Mahachaitya*, Kathmandu: *Swayambhu Vikas Mandal*, N.S. 1098, pp. 67-69.
48. Min Bahadur Shakya: *A Short History of Buddhism in Nepal,* Lalitpur: Young Buddhist Publication, 1986, pp. 2-3; *Also see;* Min Bahadur Shakya: *Princess Bhrikuti Devi*, Dehli: Book Faith India, 1977, pp. 19-20.
49. Dhanavajra Vajracharya: *Licchavikalin Abhilekh,* Kathmandu: Nepal Asiali Adyayan Sansthan, 2030 B.S, p. 392.
50. Thomas Watters: *Yuanchwang's Travels in India*, Vol. I, New Delhi: Munshiram Manoharlal Publisher, 1973, p. 1.
51. *Majjhima Nikaya* Sutta no. 3/8/2, p. 504.
52. Buddhist mythological history is depicted in the *Swayambhu Purana*. Although it is not authentic, this text is highly revered by

Nepali Buddhists, so, almost all of the followers of Buddhism in Nepal, keep the text in their house and venerate it. For details see: Badri Ratna Vajracharya: *Swayambhu Mahapurana*, Kathmandu: Sanu Maya Tuladhar, 1103 N.S, pp 1-26.

53. Vajracharya: f. n. no. 49, pp. 320-24.
54. Dhanavajra Vajracharya and Kamal Prakash Malla: *The Gopalrajvamsavali*, Kathmandu: Nepal Research Center, 1985, pp. 28-30.
55. Hemraj Shakya: *Buddha Murti Chhagu Adhyayan*, Kathmandu: Khwaspusa, 1091 N.S., pp. 3-4.
56. Vajracharya: f. n. no. 49, pp. 77-257.
57. *Ibid.*, p. 499.
58. *Arya Sanghasyetyenena Cha Sampanah Shree Shiva Deva Vihara Chaturdesiya Bhikshu Sangha* – Pashupati Vajraghar inscription. For detail see: Vajracharya: f. n. no. 49 p. 499 and 496.
59. Vajrachrya f. n. no. 49, p. 39.
60. Jagdish Chandra Regmi: *Nepal Ko Dharmik Itihash*, Kathmandu: Ratna Pustak Bhandar, 2039, pp. 145-46; *Also see*: Shakya: f.n. no. 30, p. 33.
61. Dilli Raman Regmi: *Medieval Nepal*, Calcutta: K. L Mukhopadhyaya, 1965, p. 551.
62. Inscription of Tyagal Htole quoted in Vajracharya, f. n. no. 49, pp. 387-88, 508-10.
63. Surya Vikram Gyawali: *Nepal Upatyka Ko Madhykalin Itihas*, Kathmandu: Royal Nepal Academy, 2019 B.S., p. 284.
64. *Ibid.*
65. Manuscript entitled *Dharani Sangraha* copied in 898 N.S. by a Vajracharya of Taoh Baha.
66. Narendra Dev's Yagabaha inscription quoted in Vajracharya, f. n. no. 49, p. 505.
67. Min Bahadur Shakya: 'Historical Analysis of Monasticism in Newar Buddhism', *Voice of History*, Vol. XV, No. 1, June 2000, Kirtipur, pp. 65-80.

3

HISTORY OF NEPALESE BUDDHISM

The history of Buddhism in Nepal is basically of two types—mythological and documentary. The mythological narration pertaining to Buddhism is also regarded as very important supporting evidence for the study of Nepalese Buddhism. Although such narration deals with mythology as well as stories of the deeds and miraculous powers of Buddhist deities and the devotees, it is deeply rooted in the practical aspect of Nepalese Buddhist culture. Thus, before presenting documentary and archaeological evidence, it is necessary to examine the accounts which have a popular basis in the society. It is obvious that the former narratives have no scientific evidence to support their description and do not stand up to the challenge of scientific analysis. However, it is always helpful to make an ideal interpretation of historical contexts and the continuity of Buddhism in Nepalese society through the belief of its followers. This continuity has remained unbroken since ancient times. The mythological sources of Buddhism in Nepal include narratives such as *Swayambhu Purana*, chronicles such as *Bhasavamsavali, Gopalrajvamsavali* and other *Vamsavalis*, stories and accounts of the miraculous activities of the deities, the followers and so forth. The most important sources for gaining knowledge about the history of Nepalese Buddhist thoughts are the inscriptions from ancient and medieval periods. These are readily available as there are hundreds of such inscriptions that mention Buddhism.

The inscriptions of the Lichhivis and the Mallas shed light on Buddhism in Nepal. The Lichhivi inscriptions opine that Buddhism was in its full-fledged form during ancient time, and was favoured by the rulers. Many kings favoured Buddhism and played an active role in its development. The inscription of Kings Mana Deva, Shiva Deva, Narendra Deva, Jaya Deva and others provide important information about the Nepalese Buddhism of that period. Basically, the subject of such inscriptions relating to Buddhism are—the arrival of Vajrayana in Nepal, the *Mahasanghika* sect, the Buddhist *Sangha*, donations made to the *Viharas*, the consecration of deities, the cult of Avalokiteswar, Vajra Bhairav, Status of *Bhikshu Sangha* and *Bhikshuni Sangha*, jurisdiction of the *Sangha* etc. are also mentioned in the ancient and medieval inscriptions.[1] In addition to these sources, there is ample documentary evidence that sheds light on Nepalese Buddhism particularly its historical development, literature, ritual activities, deities, practices, etc. These sources are mainly preserved in the manuscripts and traditional book (*thyasaphu*) form in the *Vajrayana Viharas*. These sources mainly belong to the medieval period. Nonetheless, these are very important sources of Nepalese Buddhism.

Nepalese Buddhism underwent notable changes during the medieval period that had far-reaching consequences. No detailed historical account has been constructed so far for the era after the Lichhivi period until the 12th century. Due to unknown reasons, sources are not available. Nonetheless, this transitional period also had an impact on Buddhism. However, we have learned about the Buddhist history of Nepal from Tibetan Sources.[2] Nepal also has inscriptions dealing with the period after the twelfth century.[3] But there are several important Tibetan sources which are related to Nepalese Buddhist history in one way or another. These very important Tibetan sources that can help Nepalese historians to reconstruct the Buddhist history of Nepal are—

- Mani-bka – bum
- Chosbyung of Bu-ston (14th century) by Buston Run chen grub (1290-1364)

- Hu-lan Deb ther (1346 A.D. by Tshak pa kun d'Gar rdo-rje (1309-1353)
- rGyal rabs gSal ba'I Me-long (1388) by -bSod nams rgyal-mtshan
- Debthar Ngon Po (The Blue Annals) of Gos lotsaba (1476) by- Gos gZhonupal.
- Deb ther Karpo (the White Annals) by dGe- 'dun Chos-Phel, and rGya bza' baz'I rNam thar by Chintey Chodak

Regarding the indigenous sources of the period, the book entitled *Documents from Rudravarna Mahavihara* has a little information regarding that period. Some documents of *Rudravarna Mahavihara* dated N.S.(Nepal *Samvat* > Newar *Samvat*) 135 to N.S. 500 are included in it. It gives valuable information on Buddhist history as well as other aspects of Nepalese Buddhism.[4]

The Mythological Accounts

Documentary evidence is found in Nepal that deals with its antiquity. The oldest excavated documents are in the form of inscriptions belonging to the Lichhivi period. Those inscriptions provide valuable information about Buddhism of that time, but one of the very important aspects of Buddhism in Nepal is that the Nepalese Buddhists have faith in the mythological tradition. Although such mythology still requires some determination of historical authenticity, the belief itself has become a part of the religious practice of Nepalese Buddhists. Therefore, they venerate such kinds of beliefs as well as the texts also.

The accounts given in the *Swayambhu Purana*[5] and *Bhasha Vamsavali*[6] give information on the early history of Buddhism in Nepal. The origin of *Swayambhu* or the *Adi Buddha* (the primordial Buddha) is not the origin of history itself but the creation of the mind through the belief pattern of Nepalese Buddhists, which received the respect of Buddhist laity to a greater extent.

Similarly, the narrative of *Bhasha Vamsavali* in relation to Buddhism of Nepal, particularly the section about Matsyendranath, the Bodhisattva of compassion, is merely a compilation of stories rather than a part of Buddhist history.

The *Swayambhu Purana* is one of the most important religious texts in Nepal, and is very sacred for Nepalese Buddhists. The text as such brought about perceptible changes in the religious life of Nepalese Buddhists. The primordial Buddha or the *Swayambhu* (the self-sprouted) is highly venerated in the Buddhist society of Nepal. The concept of the seven Buddhas (*Saptatathagata*- Vipassi, Sikhi, Vishwabhu, Kakruchhanda, Kanakmuni, Kasyahapa and Shakyamuni) is highlighted in the *Purana*.[7] Nepalese Buddhists not only venerate the seven Buddhas, but also the text of the *Swayambhu Purana* itself. The names of the seven Buddhas mentioned in the *Purana* are identical to the names mentioned in the *Buddhavamsha*.[8] The existence of some of the seven Buddhas has been archaeologically proved.[9] Huen-T-sang, a famous Chinese traveller also saw *Chaityas* erected in the memory of Kashyapa, Kanakmuni and Kakruchhanda Buddha.[10] His account obviously proved the existence of the Buddhas in different epochs before that of the historical Buddha. The account is not myth but the historical fact. The Ashokan pillar of Lumbini also mentions the Kanakmuni and Kakruchhanda Buddhas. It proves the existence of the Buddhas in different epochs before the historical Buddha.

The Buddhist society of Nepal has a long oral tradition regarding Buddha and Buddhist history. This legendary tradition has not yet been historically proved, however, people have a staunch belief in it. As concerns the history of Buddhism of Nepal, there are four very important legends which are still prevalent among the Buddhists in this country.

The story of origin of *Swayambhu* Chaitya is the starting point in the history of the origin of Buddhism in Nepal. According to the story depicted in the *Swayambhu Purana*—the *Swayambhu* is self-originated from an eternal light in a lotus flower grown in the lake in Kathmandu valley called the *Naghrada*. Finally, the lotus flower bent and landed on the *Gosringa Parvat* situated on the west. It is said that the *Gosringa Parvat* is the present day *Swayambhu* hill. At present, there is a chaitya at the top of the hill which is a popular sacred destination for Nepalese as well as the Tibetan Buddhists.

Swayambhu literally means the self bloomed. It is said to be the primordial Buddha or the Supreme Buddha. The first available inscription in the area is from the year N.S. 492 (1289 A.D) which refers to the renovation of the Stupa.[11] Nepalese Buddhists believe that *Swayambhu* is the primordial Buddha who appeared as a lotus blooming afloat on the water. It emerged out of nothing. While Manjusri drained out the water of the lake, the lotus was found standing on a small hillock called *Gosringa* or *Gopuchha Parvat.* The *Adi Buddha* is considered to be formless and omnipresent as well as the creator. *Gunakarandavyuha Sutra* mentioned the *Adi Buddha*, who is similar to *Swayambhu.*[12] Since *Gopalrajvamsavali* has not discussed the term *Swayambhu;* D.R. Regmi, a noted historian of Nepal, is of the opinion that *Swayambhu* was associated with the *Adi Buddha* only in the early 15th century.[13] However, Nepalese Buddhists, without a doubt regard *Swayambhu* as the primordial Buddha. It has occupied a significant place in the religion of the people, but in terms of historical interpretation, the authenticity of its origin is not supported by historical documents. It should be revealed as a reflection of religious beliefs of the people. The oldest inscription found at *Swayambhu* deals with the donation of land made to the *Vihara* and the performance of the fire sacrifice (the *Homa* or *Yajna)* rituals.[14]

The *Swayambhu Purana* is the oldest Nepalese Buddhist text. Its main purpose is to glorify the sacred Buddhist shrines of Kathmandu Valley and to highlight the shrine of *Swayambhu Mahachaitya.*[15]

In the sequence of legends pertaining to Shakyamuni Buddha, the story of his visit to Kathmandu is very popular among the Nepalese Buddhists. The *Swayambhu Purana* mentions that Shakyamuni Buddha came to Nepal *Mandala* from *Jetavan Vihara* at Sravasti to pay homage to the *Swayambhu Jyoti* (light) with the assembly of the 500 *Bhikshus* of the *Parvatasthana* at *Gosringa Parvat.*[16] This event is recorded by Daniel Wright in his *Vamsavali.* The Wright *Vamsavali* states that:[17]

> *During his reign (King Jitedasti) Shakya Singh Buddha came to Nepal from a city named Kapilvastu, and having visited Swayambhu Chaitya and Manjusri Chaitya, fixed his abode at Puchhagra Chaitya. While*

> *there, he accepted the worship and offerings of Chuda*[18]*, a female Bhikshu, and made 1350 proselytes, viz. Sariputra, Mahamaudgalyayana, Ananda and others from Brahman and Chhetri castes. To several Bodhisattvas such as Maitreya, and gods such as Brahma, who came to Nepal expressly to see him. Shakya described the glory of Swayambhu. He then visited Gujesvari, and after that the Namo Buddha mountain. Here he discovered and showed to his disciples certain ornaments belonging to himself, buried under a Chaitya. When he formerly existed as a prince named Mahasattva (the son of Maharath of Panauti formerly called Panchaba), he had buried these ornaments, after destroying himself by giving his flesh to a tiger to eat. He replaced them as they were and repaired the Chaitya. He next ascended into heaven and returned after his birth. Then, after preaching his doctrine to the people, he saw that the time of his death was approaching and went to a city called Kusi. Here while he was preaching to an assembly of gods (such a Brahma) and Bhiksus (such as Ananda) he disappeared. Some of his followers remained in Nepal and professed his religion.*

This statement further attests the fact that Shakyamuni Buddha visited Kathmandu and preached Buddhism at *Puchhagra Chaitya* in *Swayambhu*. A very interesting factor mentioned so far in the *Vamsavali* is that the Buddha gave *Prabajya Sambar* to 1350 people including Chuda and also gave teachings.[19] The *Yama-Niyama Shuchishantiparivarta* in the *Lalitvistara Sutra* stated that Buddha resided at *Gopuchha Parvat* for a certain period in order to pay homage to *Swayambhu* and delivered teachings to his disciples. From there, he went to *Panchaladesha.*[20] Here Buddha is said to have explained *Nepal Mahatmya* (Glorification of Nepal), and paid homage to *Swayambhu*. He also paid homage to *Guhyeswari* and received consecration, which he explained to *Bhikshu* Ananda.[21] According to all Buddhist traditions, it is normally believed that Buddha visited that place. The Srilankan as well as Myanmar Buddhists also believe that Buddha visited Srilanka and Myanmar several times. There are testimonial narratives depicted in the classical Buddhist texts to support these types of popular belief.[22] Buddha's visit to the Himalayan region is also narrated in *Avadana* literature as well as *Pali* texts.[23] Taking into consideration all such narratives and Buddha's so-called visits to Sri Lanka all the way from Mansarovar in Tibet, which adjoins present day Nepal's western Himalayas, as well as his visit to Yangoon, some Nepalese scholars hypothesized the possibility of his visit to Kathmandu. Those who supported these views say that the possibility that Buddha visited Kathmandu Valley is very likely.[24] But there is no historical evidence to support this statement, so this historical narrative cannot be considered to be authentic. It is merely a speculation or popular belief. This statement as such has no historical value in terms of authenticity. On the paradigm of historical methodology, this statement cannot be confirmed as a historical fact. However, there is no doubt that people believe that Buddha arrived in Kathmandu. History and faith are different things. Due to its lack of authenticity, it has continued to be that is presented as history.

Emperor Ashoka's Visit

The other important step in Nepal's Buddhist history is the visit of Mauryan Emperor Ashoka to Kapilvastu and Kathmandu. He was a great Buddhist, and practiced Buddhism during his rule. He made pilgrimages to the popular Buddhist shrines and Buddhist sites. He visited Lumbini which is proved by the pillar inscriptions found there and in Niglisagar in the Western Terai of Nepal. These Ashokan pillars commemorate Ashoka's pilgrimage to these places. Both these places are sacred to Lumbini is a holy place because Buddha was born there, whereas Niglisagar contained a stupa enshrining relics of Kanakmuni Buddha. He is regarded by the Buddhists as one of the former Buddhas.[25] Ashoka's visit to these places has already been verified. The pillar inscriptions attest to the fact that Emperor Ashoka visited Niglihawa. He paid homage to Kanakmuni Buddha, enlarged his stupa, and erected a stone pillar there. He also visited the Lumbini garden and worshipped Buddha there. He setup another stone pillar to declare that Buddha was born there.[26] The Nepalese Buddhist tradition also believe that Emperor Ashoka visited Kathmandu Valley as well, but his unconfirmed visit to

Kathmandu as described in Wright's chronicle and other sources, is without evidence to support it.

Regarding his visit to Kathmandu, Wright's chronicle states—

> *In the reign of Raja Asika (Ashoka), the Raja of Patliputra having heard the fame of Nepal as a sacred place, and having obtained the permission of his spiritual guide, Upagupta Bhikshu, came on a pilgrimage to Nepal accompanied by his family and followed by a large number of his subjects. He visited every holy place and bathed in every sacred water, and went to Swayambhu, Guhjeswari and eight Bauddha bitaragas or Chaityas. He also built several Chaityas. His daughter Charumati, while playing one day saw an iron arrow head turned into stone by a god; and determined to remain in Nepal, having concluded from this that it was a land of miracles wrought by the gods. The Raja, therefore, gave her in marriage to a descendant of a Chhetri named Devapala ... becoming aged Devapala and Charumati determined to pass the rest of their life in retirement. They, therefore, resolved each to build a Vihara. That of Charumati was first completed, and she died in it after living a life of Bhikshuni. All this happened in the reign of Kiranti Raja Sthunko."*[27]

This description of the chronicle tries to explain that Ashoka came to Nepal for a pilgrimage alongwith a large retinue of family and successors. He visited holy places in Kathmandu. He also built several Chaityas there. The four ancient style Chaityas in Patan (*Imadol, Lagankhel, Pulchowk* and *Pimbahal*) are said to have been established by him during his visit.

Some historians believe there is a strong possibility that Ashoka visited Kathmandu. However, it is impossible to speak in the absence of historical evidence. David Snellgrove and John K. Locke did not refute this idea. Snellgrove opines that Khotan had preserved the Buddhist tradition started by an imaginary son of Ashoka, known as Kustana. If the activities of Ashoka could reach a remote place like Khotan, with Nepal in his political domain, one should not be surprised that Ashoka visited Kathmandu and established the city of Patan. It is likely in this context that he built four great stupas in the four cardinal directions.[28] But Babu Ram Acharya, an eminent historian of Nepal, is of the opinion that the *Kirant* kings adapted Buddhism and built Ashokan Stupas at the four corners of Patan.[29]

Thus, he believed it is highly possible that Ashoka visited Kathmandu. John K. Locke agrees with this.[30] Nonetheless, it is only a historical probability. Unless we find evidence to prove that Ashoka visited Kathmandu, it cannot be confirmed as a historical fact. Even so, Ashoka's contribution to the development of Buddhism in Nepal cannot be downplayed in any way. Regarding the story of his daughter Charumati, who came to Kathmandu and married a Nepalese Prince, historians doubt her existence. References to Charumati are not found in any of the Ashokan inscriptions, edicts or Pali canons. This situation created further ambiguity and confusion in terms of historical description of Charumati in the history of Buddhism in Nepal.

As concerns the introduction of Buddhism in the Kathmandu valley, we have to depend on legends. There is no clear idea about how Buddhism came to Nepal, but according to legends, Buddhism came to Kathmandu even before the time of Gautam Buddha.[31] However, history refutes this kind of idea. Although *Swayambhu* is said to have originated as the primordial Buddha in the distant past, modern historians confirmed that *Swayambhu* Chaitya was established by Vishwa (Vrisha) Deva, a Lichhivi king.[32] If it became a place of Buddhist pilgrimage when it was established by Vishwa Deva, this contradicts the idea that Buddhism was introduced in Nepal before the time of Gautam Buddha. At any rate, the tradition and legends of *Swayambhu* cannot be equated with history and it is thereby impossible to establish the historical authenticity of such accounts.

Since Nepal is located within close proximity to India, the Buddhist creed could have come to Nepal at anytime in ancient history. There are some references to Nepal in certain Indian classical texts. The *Mulasarvastivada Vinaya* mentions Nepal in a section relating to wool trading. It mentions that a group of Bhikshus stayed at Sravasti *en route* to Nepal.[33] This text also mentions Ven. Ananda as the resident of Kathmandu who visited his birthplace to see the neighbours. As he returned from Kathmandu to Shravasti with frost bitten toes, Buddha permitted the monks to wear shoes in order to be protected from such accidents.

The account of *Mulasarvastivad Vinaya* supports the claim that Nepal was already exposed to Buddhism or to Buddhist communities.[34] If this is the case, then Buddhism could have had an impact on Nepal, and if so, people probably would have been acquainted with Buddhist creeds also.

Without historical evidence, historians have no choice except to guess how Buddhism was introduced in Nepal. The mythology regarding the introduction of Buddhism in Nepal is very popular among the Buddhist laity in Nepal even until the present time. As a result, they strongly believe in the truth of Buddha's historical visit, as well as that of other Buddhas, including Manjushri. This belief is strongly tied to the religious beliefs of ordinary followers.

The Lichhivi inscriptions attest to the fact that Buddhism was fully developed in Nepal by the later part of the ancient period,[35] but no dependable historical sources have been found so far to authenticate the historical imagination that Buddhism was introduced in Nepal even before the time of the historical Buddha. It is merely an oral tradition of the Buddhists of Nepal. The visit of Shakyamuni Buddha and Emperor Ashoka to Kathmandu are over emphasized and exaggerated in legendary accounts of Nepalese Buddhism, although no historical evidence supports this hearsay and accounts. They have historical bearings whatsoever.

Gum *Vihara*, on the other hand, is the oldest form of evidence of Buddhism in Nepal. It was a *Vihara* which was established in ancient times and it is said to be the oldest *Vihara* in Nepal. This *Vihara* was very popular during the ancient times. Historians suggest that the term *Gum* belongs to the Kirant language.[36] With lack of other evidence, the existing sources support the notion that Buddhism entered Nepal during the *Kiranti* rule, when Gum *Vihara* was established. Dhanavajra Vajracharya, a noted native historian, believes that *Hinayana* Buddhism came to Nepal around the end of *Kirant* rule.[37] The ancient inscription found in Sankhu near the *Vihara* confirms the existence of the *Mahasanghika Bhikshu Sangha.* This is very important historical evidence for piecing together the history of Buddhism in Nepal.

The Lichhivi Period

The attitude and policies of Lichhivi rulers towards Buddhism continued to play a prominent role in the development of Buddhism. It is supposedly called the golden age in the growth of Buddhist history in Nepal. The co-operative attitude of the Lichhivi rulers finally provided a basis for the overall development of Buddhism in ancient Nepal.

While writing about the history of Buddhism in Nepal, emphasis should be given to the policies adopted by ancient kings like Mana Deva, Shivadeva, Narendra Deva, Amshuvarma, Vrisha Deva and others. Even before them, there was already a *Vihara* which was very famous during that time. The *Vihara* was called Gum *Vihara*, and is a pre-Lichhivi historical *Vihara* of Nepal which is mentioned in various historical documents, including the *Gopalrajavamsavali* as well as other inscriptions. The *Vamsavali* mentions[38]—

> *Mana Deva...mahaghorapapa kritena maharodamana bhramitva Gum Vihara Sikhare tapa kritan. Tapo prabhava mahacheta mutpaddyatepratisthitasca.*

(Due to the sin committed by Mana Deva, he sat meditating in Gum *Vihara*. As a result a great Chaitya was created and consecrated.)

This proves the fact that it had already become a popular monastery by the time of Mana Deva, and was considered to be the most distinguished *Vihara*. It was established during *Kiranti* rule.[39] It was the first Buddhist *Vihara* to be established in the Kathmandu valley, and was very famous during Amshuvarma's time.[40]

It is also said that the term *Gubhaju* refers to those who were ordained at Gum *Vihara*. They were called *Gum bahalju*. This terminology was later changed to *Gubhaju,* which literally means a respected person from Gum *Vihara*. Gum *Vihara* has also played a significant role in the development of Vajrayana Buddhism in Nepal.[41] As mentioned earlier, it is a *Vihara* from the *Kiranti* period. Some historians, however, have mistakenly believed it to have been built by King Vrisha Deva of Lichhivi dynasty.[42]

It is obvious that Buddhism entered Nepal sometime before

the establishment of Gum *Vihara*. In fact, as mentioned in the *Mulasarvastivada Vinaya*, Nepal was known to some *Bhikshus* living outside Nepal at the time of Gautam Buddha, but we have no supporting evidence to prove that Buddhism was introduced to Nepal during Buddha's life time. It can only be assumed that it entered Nepal before the time of the historical Buddha in the light of relevant events and mythological traditions, which lack historical evidence.

History cannot be based on religious sentiments. All the prevailing myths and legends of Nepalese traditions relating to the Buddha and Buddhism in Nepal are the product of Nepalese people's religious beliefs. Certainly it has religious value which is ingrained in the belief system of the Buddhist people of Nepal. Nevertheless, it cannot be regarded as a historical fact.

Dhanavajra Vajracharya, a noted historian of Nepal, is of the opinion that Buddhism came to Nepal during the *Kirant* period, but historically, Buddhism was well-developed and accepted in Nepal under the Lichhivis. Available documentary evidence mentions that a large number of *Viharas*, *Bhikshuni* and *Bhikshu Sanghas* and the *Mahasanghika* and *Vajrayana* faiths have existed in Nepal ever since the Lichhivi period. In fact, Buddhism became so popular during the period that a large number of devotees made lavish donations in the name of Buddhism.

The Lichhivi rulers played a significant role in the spread of Buddhism in Nepal. Some of the rulers, especially Vrisha Deva, Narendra Deva, Amshuvarma and Shivadeva were very prominent in this respect. They made great contribution to the spread of Buddhism in one way or another. A chronicle of Nepal entitled *Gopalrajamsavali* mentions several Lichhivi Kings, such as Vrisha Deva, Amshuvarma, Dharma Deva, Shivadeva and Mana Deva, in connection with the spread of Buddhism. King Vrisha Deva has been praised as the *Sugata Shashana Pakshyapati* (the patron of Buddha's rule) in Lichhivi inscriptions, and is referred to as one who favoured Buddhism. The Pashupati inscription of Jaya Deva II dated Samvat 157 mentions:[43]

> *Ekadasa Kshitipatinaparancha bhupam hitvantare vijayino Jaya Deva Vamna Srimanbabhuva Vrisha Deva eti pratito rajottama sugatashashana Pakshyapati.*

(After twelve kings from the reign of victorious Jaya Deva II, there enthroned the best king, Vrisha Deva, who is devoted to Buddhism).

The *Changunarayan* pillar inscription of Mana Deva also mentions the deeds of King Vrisha Deva. He is referred as a king less interested in wars. He is also mentioned as a man of destiny who was faithful to his words. The text mentions:

> *(Srima) ccaru (a) yaptatapabibha (vairabbya) amasangleshepa krit (raja) bhud Vrisha Deva ityanu (Pama sa) tyapratijno daya.*[44]

The Pashupati inscription of Jaya Deva II proves that he favoured Buddhism very much. He also constructed Swayambhu Chaitya.[45] *Bhasavamsavali* further mentions that King Vrisha Deva constructed Manjubahal which is known as *Dhando* Chaitya.[46] Chabahil Chaitya was popularly known as *Dhando* during the medieval period.[47] The inscription placed in this Chaitya is dated older than the Changunarayan inscription of Mana Deva.[48]

Wright's *Vamsavali* also mentions King Vrisha Deva.[49] It states—

> *He was a pious king. He daily fed Vajrayogini, before taking his own meals. He repaired the Chaitya built by Dharmadatta (Dharma Deva Chaitya), and built several Viharas for Bhikshus to live in. He was one day to visit one of the four large Chaityas which were built on the anniversary of the commencement of the Satyayuga and being struck by severe illness, he died there. The servants of Yama took him to their master's kingdom; but Yama, when he saw him, chided them for having brought such a virtuous man to hell. He was therefore released, and restored to life again. He then compared what he had seen in Hell with what was written about it in the Karandavyuha, and finding that they agreed, he was pleased... he placed an image of Pancha Buddha near Godavari, calling the place by the name of Bandya gaon.*

After Vrisha Deva, there were some other Lichhivi kings who were also connected with Buddhism in ancient times in one way or another.

During the Lichhivi period, the most important aspect of Buddhism was that it was organized around the *Bhikshu* and *Bhikshuni Sangha*. The Lichhivi inscriptions mention different *Sanghas* such as—the *Arya Bhikshu Sangha* and *Arya Bhikshuni Sangha*. The rulers constructed *Vihara* and granted land and gave donations to the *Sangha* for its survival. In fact, it had been a pious act to make donations to the *Sangha*.[50] The Hadigaon inscription of Amshuvarma listed several *Viharas* as recipients of donations provided by the king.[51] Similarly, some of the *Bhikshu Sanghas* were given significant rights as well. The Pashupati Vajraghar and Yagabahal inscriptions of the Lichhivis mention the rights delegated to the *Sangha* of *Sri Shiva Deva Vihara*.[52] The rights granted until that time were very significant, and made the *Sangha* very powerful as well as popular among the people.

The term *Sangha* is referred in the following Lichhivi inscriptions:

Chabahil inscription[53]

Sanghasya bhaktyartha Pujarthanca Mahamune...

This inscription explains an endowment for the purpose of providing food to the *Bhikshu Sangha*. This inscription is thought to be from Vrisha Deva's time. The *Bhikshu Sangha* already became popular and well organized in Nepal by this time.

The Hadigaon inscription of Amshuvarma is very important regarding the history of Buddhist *Vihara* in Nepal. It describes the donations granted by the ruler to the prominent *Viharas*. The *Viharas* were given grants of 6 *Purana* 2 *pana* which is equivalent to the grant amount designated to Pashupatinath. The amount given to the *Viharas* is as follows—

Gum *Vihara*	—	6 Purana 2 pana
Sriman *Vihara*	—	6 Purana 2 Pana
Sri Raj *Vihara*	—	6 Purana 2 Pana
Kharjurika *Vihara*	—	6 Purana 2 Pana
Madhyama *Vihara*	—	6 Purana 2 Pana
Ordinary *Viharas*	—	3 Purana 1 Pana [54]

Chapatatole Inscription

> *Gandhakuti pratisanskara naya tadprayojane ca caturbiwsha Mahayana Pratipannarya Bhikshuni Sangha paribhogayakshyayanibi pratipadita...*

This inscription is about an endowment which was dedicated for the renovation of the main shrine and for feeding the *Bhikshuni Sangha*. It was a *Mahayana Bhikshuni Sangha*.[55]

Bandahiti inscription

> *Bhagabatasyavalokitesvarasya dhupa dipina ma 2 Aryasanghasya ca ma 5.*

(2 *manika* to offer lights to Aryavalokitesvara, and 5 manika for *Aryasangha*). It helps to know that Bodhisattva Avalokiteswar had already become very popular by Amshuvarma's time.

This inscription explains that the Avalokiteswar cult already became very popular in Nepal during the Lichhivi period. So generous devotees donated land for the management of the *Pujas* and to provide food to the *Arya Bhikshu Sangha*.[56]

Brahmatole inscription

> It attests to the popularity of the Avalokiteswar cult in Nepal around Samvat 479.[57] The worship of Avalokiteswar became popular in ancient Nepal.

The ancient inscriptions found at Yagabahal and Pashupati Vajraghara, are very important in the analysis of the Buddhist history of Nepal. These inscriptions are identical in content. According to these inscriptions—

1. The amount collected in fines for different crimes (100 pana to remove deceased foetus from the womb of a deceased pregnant woman, 3 Purana 3 Pana penalty to those who did not take care of cattle, confiscated property of those involved in five big crimes (*Pancha Mahapapa*). The confiscated properties were given to the *Arya Bhikshu Sangha* of Sri Shiva Deva *Vihara*.[58] Similarly, Shiva Deva *Vihara Sangha* was entrusted with managing the water tap in the Pashupati temple area.

2. This *Sangha* was granted with *Birta* (tax exempt privileged land tenure) land.
3. *Bhikshu Sangha* was also given limited judicial rights in order to settle minor disputes.[59]

These inscriptions also mention a large number of *Viharas* including very famous *Viharas* such as Madhyama *Vihara*, Raj *Vihara*, Abhayaruci *Vihara*, Chaturbhalasan Vartakalyanagupta *Vihara* and so on.[60]

The Lichhivi inscription found at Musumbahal in Kathmandu mentioned—

> *Sarvasattva hitaya...tasya sanskara punyartham Bhikshuni Sangha Samarpita pana purana sahita ... prakalpya tat.*

(For renovation and worship *Purana* and *Pana* are donated to the *Bhikshuni Sangha*).

It has already been proved that *Bhikshuni Sangha* was a well established institution in the ancient times, but no reference to the *Bhikshuni Sangha* have been found among the historical descriptions and evidence of the medieval period.[61] Thus, it may be assumed that the well-developed and patronized *Bhikshuni Sangha* did not exist in the medieval times, but the reason is still unknown.

The *Sankhu inscription* of Lichhivi period is regarded as very important historical evidence for the study of history of Nepalese Buddhism. Although it is in a fragmented state, but it provides information about the Mahasanghika monks of Nepal. Therefore, it has enormous historical value.[62]

The text of the fragmented Sankhu inscription is as follows—

deyadharmoyam Sridharmarajikamatya

... ... *Sanghikabhikshu Sanghasya*... ...

It mentions the existence of the *Sangha* that belonged to the *Mahasanghika* sect of Buddhism, and proves the antiquity of Buddhism in this area. Not only the *Bhikshu* lineage, but also a lineage of Mahasanghika *Bhikshuni* lineage functioned well. An inscription discovered in Bhaktapur also mentioned a Mahasanghika

Bhikshuni lineage, which existed in the area. In fact, various inscriptions found in Patan referred to the *Arya Bhikshuni Sangha*, and a newly discovered ancient inscription at Chyamasingha in Bhaktapur also mentioned the *Mahasanghika Bhikshuni Sangha*. It has been considered to be very important because it identified Nepal's ancient *Bhikshuni Sangha,* which was organized according to the Mahasanghika Vinaya lineage.[63]

These citations prove that the *Sangha* was very popular in ancient Nepal. It was a place for women to take refuge for their spiritual quest against worldly sufferings. An aspirant usually renounced the worldly society for spiritual purposes. The *Sangha* provided leadership to the entire movement. From the date of the Chabahil inscription, the word *Sangha* is referred to repeatedly in various other Lichhivi inscriptions. The *Sangha* community remained so popular and sacred that they were occasionally entrusted with minor judicial rights also. All such descriptions found in ancient inscriptions prove that the Buddhist *Viharas* were active centers of Buddhist activities in ancient Nepal.[64]

Both the *Bhikshu* and *Bhikshuni Sangha* operated side by side. We have ample evidence to support this fact.[65] Most of the prominent ancient *Viharas* were located in and around the Patan area. The *Yagabahal* inscription mentions famous *Viharas* such as *Sri Raj Vihara*, *Madhyama Vihara*, *Abhayaruchi Vihara*, *Chaturbhalatasana Vihara*, *Vartakalyana Vihara*, while describing areas of *Gullatanga grama* (present *Guita* in Patan). All these *Vihars* were located in what was then the South-east area of Patan.[66]

The Lichhivi period is regarded as the golden period in the Buddhist history of Nepal, which made it possible for Buddhism to flourish. The most important fact to be noted here is that religious syncretism was an important feature of the society of that time. Many religions and religious cults had an equal opportunity to flourish side by side. Therefore, Buddhism became a very popular and well established religion in Nepal, available inscriptions attest this fact. Many rulers had faith in Buddhism that is why some of them favoured Buddhism and provided opportunities as well as material support to flourish.

A large number of *Viharas* existed during the Lichhivi period, when the *Bhikshu* and *Bhikshuni Sanghas* were formed. In fact, there were two kinds of followers; (*i*) those who renounced worldly desire and became monks, and (*ii*) the community of household *Acharyas* or the lay *Upasakas*. The following description of Wright's chronicle further proves this fact. It states that[67]—

> *Bhaskar Varma entrusted daily worship, and the ceremonies accompanying it (of Pashupati), to Buddhamargi householder Acharyas. The rules and ceremonies to be observed he caused to be engraved on a copper plate, which he lodged with the Bhikshus of Charumiti Vihara.*

The available inscriptions do not mention specific Buddhist sects that remained dominant in Nepal. The *Sankhu* inscription alone mentioned the *Mahasanghika Bhikshu Sangha* and *Amshuvarma's Gokarna* inscription mentions the term Vajrayana. The names of deities, such as Dharmaraja *Lokeshwore*, Yamantaka, *Pancha* Buddha etc. are mentioned in different inscriptions. This proves that Buddhism in ancient Nepal largely followed the *Mahayana* tradition.[68]

The prevalence of Avlokiteswar images in many places in Nepal and tradition of placing these images in public places by individual donors as an act of merit is proof of the development of *Mahayana* Buddhism in ancient Nepal. The huge image of Avlokitcswar, which was placed in *Samvat* 180 by *Dharmajiva* is considered to be very important in the Buddhist history of Nepal. This is mentioned in the Yangabahi inscription,[69] and proves that the cult of Avlokiteswar became very popular among the Buddhist laity.

During the first half of the seventh century, Vajrayana deities became popular among Nepalese Buddhists. Deities such as Swayambhu, Vajrayogini, and Shakyamuni Buddha, are repeatedly referred to in ancient inscriptions. Similarly, *Pancha* Buddha (five celestial Buddhas), Manjushri, Vimalakirti, Samantabhadra, and Samantakusum are frequently referred to in the Lichhivi inscriptions. Those inscriptions are sufficient evidence to prove the root of Vajrayana Buddhism in ancient Nepal.[70] It is said that King

Shiva Deva was also given the *Achaluyegu abhisheka*, a tantric initiation in the Vajrayana tradition.[71]

Before this time, Shankaracharya, a devout Hindu monastic of one of the four *Pithas* in India, came to Nepal. It is said that Buddhists were persecuted by him and he compelled the *Bhikshunis* to get married. He also destroyed 84,000 texts of different kinds written about Buddhism in order to popularize the Shaivite sect of Hindu religion.[72]

There is a legend about the Shankaracharya in Nepal, according to which the Buddhists defeated six incarnations of him in religious debate. While he was being reborn for the seventh time, the sixteen Bodhisattvas who had been in India fled to the north, possibly into Nepal. Later on, he also came to Nepal and defeated them in a debate. After that, some were put to death and others fled from there. At that time there were three types of Buddhists—*Bhikshus*, *Sravakas*, and the householder *Upasakas*. A historical source mentions that no *Bhikshus* and *Sravaskas* were able to debate with Shankaracharya, but some of the lay Buddhists prepared to debate. Finally, they were defeated and some of them were put to death.[73] He is said to have ordered the *Bhikshunis* to marry and forced the laymen to shave off the knot of hair on the crown of their heads while performing the *Chudakarma*. It is also said that he put an end to many of their religious ceremonies. He also persecuted Buddhists at Manichuda mountain,[74] which was in place of Shankaracharya's triumph over the Buddhists of Nepal.

During that time, Pashupati shrine was under the control of the Buddhists. They considered Pashupatinath to be *Avlokiteswar*,[75] and also celebrated Buddha's birthday (*Buddha Jayanti*) right at the shrine. Shankaracharya retook the shrine from the Buddhists and brought Nambudari Brahmins from Kerala in India to serve as priests of Pashupatinath.

Then he turned his attention towards the Buddhist monastic centers which were considered to be corrupt and whose practitioners engaged in sexo-yogic tantric practices. It is also said that the Buddhists had sex lives.[76] Finally, they were compelled to give up false monkhood and those who had been celibate were forced to abandon celibacy.[77] Nepal, being weak in the knowledge of Buddhism, lacked the ability to face the philosophical and intellectual onslaughts of Shankaracharya, but there is no epigraphic or other documentary evidence to support his visit, nor the claims that he persecuted the Buddhists of Nepal. Only traditional beliefs support this view. Rajendra Ram opines that Buddhism remained free from adversity in the Kathmandu Valley, but the Buddhists of Nepal could not make any significant progress during this period.[78]

Although Buddhists were said to have undergone persecution by Shankaracharya, Buddhist thinkers in India were well prepared to encounter Hindu ideologues and ideologies. They were aware of these forces, which is made evident in *Doha* and *Charya* songs.[79] During Shankaracharya's life time, the parallel currents of thoughts of the Buddhist *Siddhas* were flowing in eastern India and Nepal. There were eightyfour *Siddhas*, who had an enormous impact on *Vajrayana* Buddhism. Buddhism flourished in ancient Nepal under these circumstances which were very favourable for its progress.

At present, Nepalese Buddhism is predominantly of the Vajrayana lineage. Traces of Vajrayana are found in the Gokarna inscription of Amshuvarma.[80] The *Thyagaltole* inscription also provides information on its arrival.[81] These two inscriptions are invaluable in the study of Newar Vajrayana Buddhism of Nepal. The Thyagaltole inscription mentions the names of several Vajrayana deities, and similar are found in several other inscriptions as well.

THE MEDIEVAL PERIOD

Needless to say, Buddhism flourished well during the Lichhivi period, and this tradition continued in medieval times. By that time, Vajrayana became most powerful and popular form of Buddhism in the country. A large number of inscriptions are now available that describe various Buddhist activities in the Kathmandu Valley during the medieval times.

Traces of *Mahayana* Buddhism date back to the *Sankhu* inscription, whose fragmented lines provide information about the existence of the Mahasanghika *Bhikshu Sangha*.[82]

This inscription proves the presence of Mahasanaghika monks in the Sankhu area. The strength of the *Mahayana* and *Vajrayana* sects is further attested to by the inscriptions of *Chapat tole* (*Chaturbimsa Mahayana Bhikshuni Sangha*), the *Gokarna inscription* of Amshuvarma (<*Vajrayana*>) and, so on.[83]

The Lichhivi rulers gave Buddhism a proper environment in which to flourish in Nepal, and this did not change greatly at the end of the regime. The Malla rulers also had respect for Buddhism, which continued to be practiced in medieval times. The medieval inscriptions of the Malla rulers of Kathmandu Valley still exist, and provide valuable information about the history of Buddhism in Nepal.

However, no adequate sources are available for the transitional period (until the 12th century). This period is popularly known as the dark period in Nepalese history, but, enormous volumes of Sanskrit Buddhist manuscripts, which are available in Nepal (in the national archives, Asa Saphu Kuthi, Keshar Library, T.U. Library, and individual possession) and abroad (India, Tibet, Japan,, U.K, France, Germany, Russia and U.S.A) shed light on the Buddhist history of Nepal during medieval times.[84] Archaeological evidence is available which covers the period from 13th century onwards and sheds light on the history of Buddhism in Nepal.[85]

Dhanavajra Vajracharya's medieval inscriptions only date from the early 16th century, but some other sources refer to evidence from earlier periods.[86] Those inscriptions, in fact provide invaluable information on Buddhist history, rituals, practices, *Viharas*, the tradition of offering donations, the installation of statues of new deities, the monks and their status, *Brahmacharya Bhikshu*, hundred thousand Chaityas, *Vihara Guthi*, *Gandhuri* (*Kwapadyo* shrine) ritual consecration, various rules on Buddhist practices, *Puja*, renovations of sacred structures, participation in rituals, and various similar acts. Most of those medieval inscriptions mention contemporary *Viharas* once famous in their area.

The medieval (Buddhist) *Viharas* of Newar Vajrayana tradition remained very important in Buddhism.[87] Their role in the continuity and preservation of Buddhist rituals as well as in recitation practices is vital. However, the Newar Buddhists of the later Malla period are responsible for the degradation of Buddhist practices. In fact, they are accused of ruining Nepal's once highly celebrated Buddhist scholastic tradition.

At that time, Buddhism was widely practiced in Nepal, but Hinduism was the dominant faith. Even so, there was antagonism against Buddhism in one way or other. Thus, thousands of Mahavihara, *Kacha Baha* and *bahil* were established and operated without hindrance. It should be noted that a *Vihara* is the microcosm of Buddhist culture. All the *Viharas* are private sanctuaries which belong to a particular lineage of Newar Buddhists. Every *Vihar* has its own *Sangha*. Members of the particular lineage group are organized within the *Sangha*. The *Bhikshu Sangha*, however, vanished long ago. Those persons whose forefathers were once monks, who continued the *Sangha* within the settlements with its members, constituted a group which was separate from those belonging to others. This group was also called the *Sangha*, as it is today.[88] Even though they performed rituals to signify their renunciation of worldly desires, they had long ago rejected the practice of celibate monasticism. Thus, Nepalese Buddhism is Buddhism without monks; it is merely Buddhism based on rituals. Every tenet of Buddhism, either philosophical or otherwise, has been transformed into a ritual including entire philosophical tenets, as well as the *Prabajya*.

Ever since medieval times, Newar Buddhists have not needed to devote themselves to the practice of *Bhumi* or *Paramita* or study higher forms of philosophical texts because the ritual practices are believed to make all such merits available to them. Thus, there is no need to practice the precepts. All these developments are the product of medieval minds and even at present Buddhist scholarship does not exist. The tradition of teacher and the disciple has been maintained to some extent, but no sign of Buddhist intelligence having the qualities of medieval scholarship can be found in the Buddhist Society of Nepal. The glorious tradition of Buddhist scholarship completely died out during the late medieval period.

A very interesting example can be cited that support this idea.

Nepal was once the center of learning for Tibetans. Tradition died out by the later Malla period. No scholars remained in the society to give teachings and satisfy the followers. When a Tibetan Lama (Kwacha Lama) came to Swayambhu and gave teaching, he was able to attract the attention of the Nepalese, from whom he also received a lot of praise, but none of the Buddhists thought to revive the glorious past and let the society remain intact.

However, it should also be mentioned that unwillingness of the Vajracharyas to impart whatever they knew (irrespective of its quality) to non-Vajracharya Buddhist groups or the non-Buddhists groups further accelerated the waning process of the scholastic tradition. It always produced a negative impact on Nepalese Buddhism.

During medieval times, Nepal played a prominent role in the spread of Buddhism. Nepal opened her doors to fugitive Buddhists who fled to Nepal after the Turkish invasion of India, causing Nepal to become the abode of fugitive Indian Buddhists.[89] Nepal benefited from the arrival of Indian scholars and monks, who brought thousands of volumes of Sanskrit literature and samples of craftwork. This era was considered to be a period of fair exchange of ideas and beliefs, but the monastic order in Nepal suffered from cultural sterility due to the metamorphosis it underwent because of the *Shaivite* reformers, who bluntly subjected the priests to the rigid influences of caste and marriage.[90]

A large number of documents from the Malla period dealing with activities related to Buddhism are available now. Those documents primarily concern the donation of various items to the Buddhist pantheons, Buddhist *Guthi*, the installation of *Dharmadhatu*, *Aagam puja*, ritual feasts, *Busadhan* ritual, renovation, various deities, consecration rituals, *Viharas* and so on. The descriptions and details of such documents deal with various Buddhist activities and devotional acts.

Buddhism was thriving, and a large number of *Vihara* were established in the Kathmandu Valley. Patan alone housed hundreds of *Vihar,* within its periphery.[91] The *Viharas* at that time were lavishly decorated and were very rich in art forms. The fact that medieval times had produced hundreds of prominent scholars of higher standing is evidence of the strength of Buddhism in the society. Those scholars were known far and wide for their scholarship in Tantra, Sadhana, Yoga, logic, philosophy, rituals, *Chacha* (*Charya*) songs, *Vidhi*, and so on.[92] Other Buddhists, mainly from Tibet, came to them for higher learning. The most famous Vajracharyas were *Mahakaruna* or *Ye rang ba*, Vagisvarakirti, Bharo, Ravindradeva and others.[93] Dharmaswami (Chaglotsaba), the great Tibetan scholar and translator was also trained in Nepal under Vajracharya *Pandits*.[94] Even *Vagisvarakirti*, a Nepalese scholar, has his own lineage from when he was a *Guru* in Tibet. These Buddhist scholars rendered a valuable service in the development of Buddhist history.

The entire tradition of Nepal's Vajrayana Buddhism, during centuries of history, gradually fell into decline. The changes were very serious and were marked by the end of celibate monastic practice as well as monkhood, and changes in ritual and initiation process etc. made a negative impact on the history of Buddhism in Nepal. The gradual decline of Newar Buddhism during the second-half of the Malla regime shaped Nepalese Buddhism into its present form.

The study of Buddhist history in Nepal cannot be limited to Kathmandu Valley, as Buddhism spread to western Nepal as well. During the period of expansion, Buddhism made inroads into hill tribes in western Nepal who were considered to be *Anarya* by the Brahmins. In fact, Buddhism became a favourite faith for those who were ill-treated by the Brahmin community. The *Khasiya* of western Nepal were one of these tribes. Buddhism also flourished to a great extent in the *Khasa* area, whose proximity to Tibet and frequent contact with Indian Buddhists paved the way for the amalgamation of the *Vajrayana* and *Lamaistic* faith. Buddhism not only became a civilizing agent for this region, but also an ideological standard for the manifestation of social status for the *Khasa* rulers.[95]

The history of Buddhism, however, is incomplete without dealing with the history of the *Theravada* tradition in Nepal. In recent times, it has developed into a more active movement. Although the historical writings of Nepalese scholars try to link it to the remote past, its history in Nepal is of recent origin. *Theravada* Buddhism has been gaining momentum in modern times, and the study of Nepalese Buddhism cannot be complete without including the Nepalese tradition of *Theravada* Buddhism. It has shown a great increase in activity since the 1940s. Since then, it has gone through several phases. At present, it even has believers among the followers of Vajrayana in Nepal. A considerable number of Shakyas and Vajracharyas started to observe the *Theravada* tradition instead of Vajrayana and its rituals. *Theravada* Buddhism has been supported by several Buddhist organizations in Sri Lanka and Thailand, and has its own Bhikshu organizations and a well organized *Pariyatti Sikshya* (traditional Buddhist education programme). Both these organizations are busy with the mission of strengthening *Theravada* Buddhism in Nepal. Since 1940, it has produced eminent practitioners, who have rendered invaluable service in the progress of *Theravada* in Nepal as well as in the development of Buddhist expertise. As a matter of fact, it has very bright prospect for the future in Nepal.

References

1. Various Lichhivi inscriptions cited in Dhanavajra Vajracharya: *Lichhavikalka Abhilekh,* Kathmandu: Institute for Nepal and Asian Studies, 2030, pp. 74-78, 185-186, 320-335, 370-371, 382-385, 387-388, 451-455, 490-491, 496-510 and 548-562.
2. Min Bahadur Shakya: *Princess Bhrikuti*, Delhi: Book Faith, 1997, pp. 7-13.
3. Dhanavajra Vajracharya has published medieval documents in his book dealing with the Patan section. The oldest document cited in this collection is the inscription of Guita bahi dated N.S. 635; Dhanavajra Vajracharya (ed.): *Madhyakalin Abhilekh*, Kirtipur: Center for Nepal and Asian Studies, B.S., 2056, pp. I-IV.
4. Bernard Kolver and Hemraj Shakya: *Documents from Rudravarna Mahavihara* Patan : *Sales and Mortgage*, Sankt: VGH Wissenschaftsverlag, 1985, pp. 32-43 and 103-211.
5. Min Bahadur Shakya and Purna Harsha Vajracharya (ed.), *Swayambhu Purana*, Lalitpur: Nagarjuna Institute of Exact Methods, 2058, pp. 28-50.

6. *Bhasavamsavali*, Vol. 2, Kathmandu: National Library, 2023, pp. 5-17.
7. Badri Ratna Vajracharya (ed.): *Sri Swayambhu Mahapurana,* Lalitpur: Jograj Shakyavamsha, 1116 N.S., pp. 9-20.
8. Shakya: f. n. no. 2, pp. 15-18; Bhuvan Lal Pradhan (tr.), *Buddhavamsha* (Newari), Kathmandu: Jnaratna Kamsakar, 2057, pp. 126-60.
9. Lumbini Pillar Inscription : quoted from D.C. Sircar, *Inscriptions of Ashoka,* New Delhi: Ministry of Information and Broadcasting, 1998, p.21.
10. N. Dutta and K.D. Bajpai: *Development of Buddhism in Uttar Pradesh*, Lucknow, Government of Uttar Pradesh, 1956, p. 322.
11. D.R. Regmi: *Medieval Nepal*, Vol. 1, Calcutta: K. L. Mukhopadhyaya, 1965, p. 565.
12. Min Bahadur Shakya (ed.): *Arya Gunakarandavyuha Sutra* (Newari), Lalitpur: Nagarjuna Institute Exact Methods, 1997, pp. 22.
13. Regmi, f. n. no. 11, p. 568.
14. Vajracharya, f. n. no. 1, pp. 74-76.
15. Shakya, f. n. no. 5.
16. Vajracharya, f. n. no. 7, pp. 3-5
17. Daniel Wright, *History of Nepal* Translated from Parbatiya, Calcutta: Sushil Gupta and Company, 1958, p. 65.
18. This name is mentioned as *Chunda* by Badri Ratna Vajracharya. f. n. no. 7, p. 4.
19. Shakya, f. n. no. 2, pp. 18-19.
20. Nisthananda Vajracharya (tr.), *Lalitvistara Sutra*, Lalitpur: Y. M. B. A., 1978, p. 577.
21. *Ibid*, pp. 577-86.
22. Wilhelm Geiger (Eng.tr.): *The Mahavamsha or the Great Chronicle of Ceylon*, New Delhi: Asian Educational Services, 1986, pp. 1-9; Bhikshu Sudarshan, *Nepalya Bauddha Dharma*, Vol. 1, Kathmandu: 1982, pp. 20.
23. For details see: Vajracharya, f. n. no. 20, pp. 587-96.
24. Shakya, f. n. no. 2, p. 18.
25. Sircar, f. n. no. 9, p. 21.
26. Niglisagar and Lumbini Ashokan pillars describe it. *See*: *Ibid*, p. 54.
27. A *Vihara* named Chabahil near Devpatan is said to have been built by Charumati.

28. David L. Snellgrove: *Tibetan Buddhism*, Vol. II, Boston: Sambhala Publications, 1987, p. 365; *Also see*: Shakya, f. n. no. 13, pp. 20-21.
29. Devi Prasad Bhandari: *'Itihas Shiromani Babu Ram Acharyaley Tayar Garnubhayeko Nepalko Sankshipta Itihas', Purnima,* Vol. 47, Year 12, No. 3, 2037 B.S., pp. 1-5.
30. For more information see John K. Locke, *Unique Features of Buddhism*, in Tadeus Skoropski (ed.), *The Buddhist Heritage*, Tring: Institute of Buddhist Studies, 1989, p. 97.
31. Vajracharya, f. n. no. 7, pp. X-XI.
32. Dhanavajra Vajracharya and Kamal Prakash Malla: *The Gopalrajvamsavali,* Kathmandu: Nepal Research Center, 1985, Folio 20 Kha 3, pp. 28 and 76.
33. Sylvan Levi: 'Le Nepal' , *Kailas* Vol. 3, No.1, 1975, p. 12; Shakya, f. n. no. 2, p. 19.
34. Mulsarvastivada Vinaya Vastu, Shakya, f. n. no. 2, pp. 16-19.
35. Hari Ram Joshi: *Nepalko Prachin Abhilekh,* Kathmandu: Royal Nepal Academy, 2030, pp. 66-70 and 293-97.
36. Dhanavajra Vajracharya: 'Gum *Vihara*', *Madhuparka*, Year 4, No. 12, 2028, pp.22-25; Bhadra Ratna Vajracharya (ed.), *Dhanavajra Vajracharyaka Aitihasik Lekh Sangraha*, Lalitpur: Hera Devi Shakya, 2056, V.S., pp. 8-10.
37. Vajracharya and Malla, f. n. no. 32, p.9.
38. Sri *Gopalrajvamsavali,* folio no. 206, *Ibid.*
39. Vajracharya, f. n. no. 1, p. 510.
40. Shankar Lal Joshi, *Amshuvarma*, New Delhi: Anmol Publication, 1993, p. 157.
41. *Ibid*.
42. *Ibid*, p. 158; Dhanavajra Vajracharya is of opinion that this is the *Kiranta* period *Vihara*. f. n. no. 32, pp. 22-25.
43. Vajracharya, f. n. no. 1, pp. 549; Joshi, f. n. no. 35, pp. 577-89.
44. Changunarayan Inscription dated 386; *Ibid*, p.10, Joshi, f. n. no. 35, pp. 6-12.
45. *Raja Vrishva Deva... Tenakrita Sinaguvihara Chaitya Bhattarika Pratishthita Sampurna Krita*. Vajracharya, *et al,* f. n. no. 27, folio 20, p. 28.
46. *Bhasavamsavali*, Vol. 1, Kathmandu : Deptt. of Archaeology, 1963, p.56.
47. Vajracharya, f. n. no. 1, p. 3; Joshi, f. n. no. 35, pp. 66-70.
48. Hari Ram Joshi, *Himjwala*, Lalitpur: The author, 2026 B.S., pp. 1-9.
49. Wright, f. n. no. 17, pp. 69-70.

50. Some famous ancient *Viharas* are—Gum *Vihara*, Sriman *Vihara*, Sivadev *Vihara*, Kharjunika *Vihara* and Ajika *Vihara*. Vajracharya, f. n. no. 1, pp. 320; Also see Rajendra Ram, *History of Buddhism in Nepal 704-1396,* Patna: Jana Bharati Prakashan, 1977, pp. 21-31.
51. Vajracharya, f. n. no. 1, pp 320-22; Joshi, f. n. no. 35, pp. 293-97; 'Hadigaon ko Amshuvarma ko Shilalekh', *Purnima* Vol. 14, Year 4, No. 2, 2024 B.S., p. 123..
52. Vajracharya, f. n. no. 1, pp. 496-506; Joshi, f. n. no. 35, pp. 508-10, 513-15; 'Patan Yagbahal ko Narendra Devako Abhilekh', *Purnima* Vol. 14, Year 4, No. 2, 2024 B.S., pp. 117-19; 'Pashupati Vajragharko Narendra Devko Abhilekh', *Purnima* Vol. 14, Year 4, No. 2, 2024 B.S. , pp. 119-21.
53. Vajracharya, f. n. no. 1, pp. 1-2; *Also see*: Ramji Tewari *et.al*, *Abhilekh Sangraha*, Kathmandu: Itihas Samshodhan Mandal, 2020 V.S., Joshi, f. n. no. 35, p. 66.
54. *Purana* and *Pana* were monetary units used in ancient times, but the real value of the unit is not yet identified. Vajracharya, f. n. no.1, pp. 320-22; Also See: Joshi, f. n. no. 35, p. 293-97; *Purnima,* f. n. no. 51.
55. Vajracharya, f. n. no. 1, pp. 382-83, Tiwari, f.n. no.53, Vol.V; Joshi, f.n. no. 35, pp. 113-15.
56. Dhanavajra Vajracharya, f. n. no.1, p. 386; Joshi, f. n. no. 35, pp. 322-24.
57. Vajracharya, f. n. no. 1, pp. 185-86; Tewari, f. n. no.53; Vol. I, Joshi, f. n. no. 35, pp. 146-47.
58. Vajracharya, f. n. no. 1, pp. 496-506; Joshi, f. n. no. 35, pp. 508-10/ 513-15.
59. Joshi, f. n. no. 35, pp. 508-19; Vajracharya, f. n. no. 1, pp. 501-06; *Purnima*, f. n. no. 52, pp. 117-21.
60. Vajracharya, f. n. no. 1, p. 320, 496-97, 505 and 540, Joshi, f. n. no. 35, pp. 293-96, 479-80, 513-15, 558 and 561.
61. Vajracharya, f. n. no. 1, p. 507.
62. *Ibid*, p. 508; Joshi, f. n. no. 35, pp. 523-25.
63. *Pasuka* Vol. II, No. 11, N.S. 1118. *Also see*: Min Bahadur Shakya, 'A Historical Analysis of Monasticism in Newar Buddhism', *Voice of History*, Vol. XV, No. 1, June 2000, Kirtipur, pp. 65-80.
64. Rajendra Ram, f. n. no. 50, pp. 91-150.
65. Tewari, f. n. no. 53, vol. V, p.8; Vajracharya, f. n. no. 1, pp. 505-10, 382 and 383; Joshi, f. n. no. 35, pp. 113, 293, 479 and 508.
66. Vajracharya, f. n. no. 1, pp. 499-501, and 505; Joshi, f. n. no. 35, pp. 513-15.

67. Wright, f. n. no. 17, p. 67.
68. Naresh Man Vajracharya: *Buddhism in Nepal*, Delhi: Eastern Book Linkers, 1998, p. 57-61.
69. See: Yagabahal Inscription, Vajracharya, f. n. no. 1, p. 591; Joshi, f. n. no. 35, pp. 622-23.
70. Vajracharya, f. n. no. 1, pp. 387-88.
71. Wright, f. n. no. 17, pp. 76-77.
72. *Ibid*, pp. 70-71.
73. *Ibid*, p.70.
74. *Ibid*, p. 71.
75. Rajendra Ram, f. n. no. 50, pp. 65-66.
76. *Ibid*, p. 66.
77. Wright, f. n. no. 17, p.71, Rajendra Ram, f. n. no. 50, pp. 66-67.
78. Rajendra Ram, f. n. no. 50, p.70-71.
79. *Ibid*.
80. Vajracharya, f. n. no. 1, pp. 370-71; Joshi, f. n. no. 35, pp. 340-42.
81. Joshi, f. n. no. 35, pp. 322-24; Vajracharya, f. n. no 1, pp. 387-88.
82. Vajracharya, f. n. no. 1, pp. 508-10; Joshi, f. n. no. 35, pp. 523-25.
83. Joshi, f. n. no. 35, p.113; Vajracharya, f. n. no. 1, pp. 370-71, 382-83.
84. For details on such Mss. see: Shanker Thapa 'Textual History of Pancharaksya Sutra in Nepal', *Voice of History*, Vol. XV, No. 2, June 2000, Kirtipur, pp. 21-38; Min Bahadur Shakya, *Preservation of Sanskrit Buddhist MSS in the Kathmandu Valley: Its Importance and Future*, Paper presented at Berkeley Buddhist Research Center, California, 1998, pp. 1-19.
85. Medieval documents dealing with Buddhism or activities of Buddhist institutions are published in Vajracharya, f. n. no. 3, pp. 1-270; Kolver and Shakya, f. n. no. 4, pp. 1-569; Joshi, f. n. no. 35, pp. 1-645.
86. Vajracharya, f. n. no. 3, p.1; Regmi, f. n. no. 11; Luciano Petech, *Medieval History of Nepal*, Rome: ISMEO, 1984, pp. 72-92. This source has quoted a manuscript entitled *Astashahasrika Prajnaparamita* dated 1199 A. D.
87. For details of role and functioning of Vajrayana Mahavihara see: Indra Kumari Vajracharya: *Cultural Heritage of Lakshmi Kalyana Varma Sanskarita Ratnakara Mahavihara of Patan*, (Unpublished Thesis submitted to PGD Buddhist Studies Programme) Tribhuvan University, 2001, pp.7-41. *Also see*: David Gellner: *Monks, Householder and Tantric Priests*, New Delhi: Foundation Books,

1996, pp. 162-80. Ranjana Vajracharya: *The Role of Hiranyavarna Mahavihara in The Socio-Cultural Life of Newar Buddhists*, (Unpublished Ph.D. dissertation), Kirtipur: T.U. Faculty of Humanities and Social Sciences, 2050 B.S; John K. Locke: *Karunamaya*, Kathmandu: Sahayogi Prakashan, 1980, pp. 9-66; Herakazi Vajracharya, *Yasodhara Mahavihara Sangha,* Lalitpur: Buddha Jayanti Samaroha Samiti, 2050, pp. 1-164.

88. D.R. Regmi: *Medieval Nepal*, Calcutta: K. L. Mukhopadhyaya, 1966, p. 776.
89. Rajendra Ram, f. n. no. 50, pp. 159-62; P. V. Bapat: *2500 Years of Buddhism*, New Delhi: Ministry of Information and Broadcasting, 1997, pp. 82-83.
90. D.R. Regmi, *Ancient Nepal*, Calcutta: K. L. Mukhopadhyaya, 1960, p. 26.
91. For list of *Viharas* with date see: Regmi, f. n. no. 11, pp. 766-75.
92. Badri Ratna Vajracharya: *Nhapayapim Prasiddha Vajracharyapim*, Kathmandu: Ananda Kuti Vihara Trust, 2046 B.S, pp. 1-41.
93. George N. Roerich, *The Blue Annals*, New Delhi: Motilal Benarsi Dass, 1996, pp. 355, 361, 375-84, 758 and 807; *Also see*: Hubert Decleer, 'Sacred Biography of Bharo-Maimed Hand A Tenth Century Bajracharya from Nepal', *Buddha Jayanti Smarika 2051 B.S.*, Lalitpur: Oku Bahal, 2051 B.S., pp. 95-104.
94. George N. Roerich: *Biography of Dharmaswamin* (Chag- Lo-tsa-ba Chos-rje- dPal), Patna: K.P. Jayaswal Institute, 1959, pp. IV- V.
95. Rajendra Ram. f. n. no. 50, p. 154.

4

GENERAL FEATURES OF NEPALESE VIHARAS

There are many Buddhist *Viharas*, popularly known as *baha, bahal* or *bahi* in the Kathmandu Valley. Most of these *Viharas* are very ancient, some of them are more than two hundred years old.[1] Those *Viharas* were established by various individuals during different historical period. There is a famous Vajrayana *Vihara* in Nepal, and some prominent *Viharas* in Patan include *the Hiranyavarna Mahavihara, Rudravarna Mahavihara, Yashodhara Mahavihara, Ratnakar Mahavihara* and so on. Bhaskar Varma, Shiva Deva, Vidyadhara Sharma and Lakshmi Kamadeva respectively established these *Viharas*. *Shakya Singha, Sumangal, Manimandap, Bishwa Shanti, Anandakuti* and *Sri Kirti Vihara* are prominent Theravadin *Viharas* at present.

There are two types of Theravadin *Viharas*—those that have their own sacred structures, and those that are housed in the Vajrayana *Kacha baha* and *bahi* complexis. The *Manimandap Vihara* and *Sumangal Vihara* of Patan are examples of the second type. The *Manimandap Vihara* shares a space in *Dauga bahi* (Patako Tole) of Patan. Similarly, the *Sumangal Vihara* is in the Yanga *baha*-Yogalakshi *Vihara*. The latter is the *Kacha baha* of *Rudravarna Mahavihara*. Both the Theravada creed and Vajrayana rituals are performed simultaneously in these *Viharas*, but at separate shrines. The *Sangha* members of *Yanga baha* also practice *Theravada* Buddhism.

In fact, there are at present 167 *Viharas* in Patan city, 140 in Kathmandu, 20 in Bhaktapur and 9 in Thimi. There are all together 440 Buddhist *Viharas* in the Kathmandu Valley, excluding 49 recent *Theravada Viharas*.[2] However, the number of *Viharas* that John K. Locke counted varies from this figure.

There are three categories of *Viharas* in Newar Buddhism. They are—

1. *Maha Vihara* (*Mu baha*)
2. *Madhyamika Vihara* (*bahi*), and
3. *Samanya Vihara* (*Kacha baha*)[3] .

1. Maha Vihara (*Mu baha*)

The *Mahavihara* is a term used to denote a Buddhist monastery where *Brahmachari Bhikshus* practiced a higher level of meditation. In these monasteries, there is a ritual to beat *Dharmagandi* four times a day as a part of the ritual. At first, this was done during meditation, but now-a-days, all of the main *Viharas* continue the tradition of beating *Dharmagandi* although they have ceased to practice meditation. This ritual is not performed in *Kacha baha* and *bahi Vihara*.

2. Madhyamika *Vihara* (*bahi*)

In this type of *Vihara*, *Brahmachari Bhikshus* lived, studied and practiced Buddhism. These are also called *bahi*. Generally, the *bahis* were built outside the city. Even though they were called *Brahmachari Bhikshus*, they did not practice celibacy after the reforms of King Jyasthiti Malla.

3. Samanya *Vihara* (*Kacha baha*):

Samanya Vihara is called *Kacha baha*. It is the branch of Mahavihara in which Buddhist *upasaka* and *upasika* practice Buddhism together. In fact, they practice three Refuge— *Panchasila*, *Dana* and *Dhyana*.

The *bahi* were mostly built outside the residential areas and the *bahi* of Patan were originally built outside the city. The location of *Puchho bahi* and *Guitah bahi* prove this hypothesis. However, these *baha* were constructed within the city.

All the *baha* and *bahi* use two names—one in Sanskrit and the other in vernacular Newari. In the local tongue, a *Vihara* is called *ba*, *baha* or *bahi*. The Newari language uses the shorter names for the *Vihara*. The term *baha* is the corrupted form of Sanskrit term *Vihara*, which denotes a Buddhist monastery.[4] Most of the *baha* are organized in such a way that *Mubaha* are affiliated with *Kacha baha* and *Nani*,; *Kacha baha* is the branch of the main *Vihara*, and *Nani* is attributed to the residential areas of the *Sangha* members. The *baha* are a little different from each other due to physical features, the pattern of rituals, the organization of the *Sangha*, its functions. Most of the *baha* and *bahi* in the Kathmandu Valley are ancient. From ancient times until the medieval period, the liberal individual donors contributed and erected various spectacular *Viharas*, but after the end of the Malla period, not a single Newar Buddhist *Vihara* was constructed in the Kathmandu Valley. It is noteworthy that Tibetan Buddhist sects established a large number of monasteries in and around Kathmandu Valley, which are lavishly decorated and ornamented.

Viharas, as the main centers of religious activities, greatly contributed to the development of religious texts, doctrinal manuscripts and Buddhist education. They also played a role of immense significance in Buddhist cultural development. In the Newar Buddhism, *Viharas* play an important role in *Sangha* functions. The latter perform extensive rites and rituals, which are an important aspect of the *Kriya* tantra (the tantra of action) practice. A *Sangha* of Buddhist followers lives in each *Vihara*, which is regulated by a set of rules within its boundary. During the long course of history, the Buddhist *Sangha* contributed to the continuity of the religious and, to some extent, philosophical tradition. Among the Vajrayana adherents in Nepal, the role of the *Sangha* has been dominant in the construction and maintenance of *Viharas* as a religious unit especially in terms of the ritual culture. *Viharas* have played a significant role in educating people and preaching Buddhist creeds. The *baha* and *bahi* in Newar Buddhism are the monasteries which have a *Sangha* of lay practitioners. The *Sangha* members refer to themselves as household *Bhikshu*, but they are lay followers of Buddhist creeds who do not renounce worldly desires in order to follow the path of a monastic life. All men of this particular lineage (*Kava)* are attached to the *baha* and *bahi* as members of the *Sangha* after performing several rites and getting initiated into the monastery for four days as *Bhikshu*.[5] The initiation ritual makes them members of the *Sangha* and also enables them to perform various rituals in the main shrine as the guardian (*Dyopala*) of the deity. However, he still must participate in more advanced rituals, religious functions and the *Vihara Guthi*. The *Vihara Sangha* of the Vajrayana tradition means the *Sangha* of lay practitioners, but not the community of celibate monks. Most of the *Sangha* members do not take Bodhisattva vows. Therefore, their practice does not seem to be compatible with the rules and practices mentioned in the *Bodhicharyavatara* of Shantideva.

It is noteworthy that Newar Buddhism is without monks; it is a Buddhism of rituals rather than of philosophy, as ritual practice is the main feature of Newar Buddhism. Non-violence is incompatible here, as certain Vajrayana rituals require animal slaughter, etc. This is very important in Newar Buddhist practice and for their identity in Buddhist society. They lack a living doctrinal tradition.[6] Only people who are initiated within the lineage can become members of the *Sangha*, and wives, daughters, and uninitiated sons are not given membership. All members remain affiliated with the *Vihara* even if they move outside its physical boundaries for residential purposes. The *barechhoegu* is performed only in *Viharas* that the fathers of *barechhoegu* candidates are affiliated with.

All the *Sangha* members are appointed as the *Dyopala* (the daily rituals performer) at the shrine of *Kwapadyo* (main deity) turn by turn. The turns start with the eldest member and descend in order. The term of a *Dyopala* is normally for one month in most of the *Viharas*. However, it is only for fifteen days at *Hakha baha*. During this period a *Dyopala* is required to follow certain specific rules. Those rules are related to the performance of the *dekhachakegu* (the opening of the worship of deities), *nitya puja* (daily worship of the guardian deity), at 8.30 A.M. a small boy walks round the locality ringing small bell, *Dharmaganthi thayegu* (to beat a hollow log-108 times) and offer *aarti* (perform an offering of lights in the evening) to the *Kwapadyo*. In most of the *baha*, the *Dyopala* usually comes in the morning and evening to open the shrine and perform the prescribed services, rituals and *puja*. In some *baha*, the *Dyopala* is required to stay at the *Vihara* complex during his tenure.[7]

Most of the *baha* in Patan have five, ten or twenty elders. They are called *Aju, thakali* or the *thayapa*. The head of the elders is called *Chakreshwore* or *Thapaju*. The *Chakreshwore* is a tantric priest, the ritual performer who performs secret tantric rituals in the *Agam kotha* (a secret room for tantric deities) in the *baha*. The committee of elders (*Aju*) of the *Sangha* decides annual programmes and approves the budget for regular *Sangha* activities. The elders play a key role in performing *barechhoygu* and *Achaluyegu* initiations for the sons of the *Sangha* members and *Chhatrarohana* and *Pancha Sthavira* initiations for older members of the *Sangha*.

Buddhist rituals such as *dana* (*Panchadana*, *Navadana*, *Samyaka Mahadana*)[8], *puja* (*Basundhara puja*, *Disipuja* etc.) and various *Guthi* activities (*Bicha Guthi, Acharya Guthi* and *Sana Guthi*) are performed and observed in all Buddhist *Viharas*.

Buddhist Viharas of Patan

The vivid imagination of the Newars has enabled them to see the layout of the city as a religious symbol. It is said that the city of Patan was originally built in the shape of a Buddhist *chakra* (wheel).[9] In the past, the city itself was bound by Dipavatinagar (Guita tole) in the east, Maitinagar or Matiko (Lagankhel) on the South, Silapuri Danagiri (Pulchowk) in the west and Lalitaramya (Kumbhesvara) in the north.[10] Patan, predominantly a Buddhist city, has a large number of Buddhist adherents and lavishly decorated and spectacular medieval Buddhist *Viharas*.

At present, there are fifteen main *Viharas* (*Mu baha*) in Patan, which have hundreds of affiliated *Kacha baha* and *nani*.

However, 3 additional *Viharas* are often added to the list. Those *baha* are[11]—

1. Bu *baha*	Vidyadhara Sharma Samskarita Yashodhara Mahavihara
2. Kwa *baha*	Bhaskara Deva Samskarita Hiranyavarna Mahavihara
3. Dhum *baha*	Gunalakshmi Samskarita Gunalakshmi Mahavihara
4. Wam *baha*	Suryavarma Samskarita Vajrakirti Mahavihara
5. Jyo *baha*	Rudradeva Nagapala Samskarita Jyoti Mahavihara
6. Su *baha*	Indra Deva Samskarita Jaya Manoharvarma Mahavihara
7. Yachu *baha*	Baladhar Gupta Samskarita Baladhar Gupta Mahavihara
8. Bhinche *baha*	Shankaradeva Samskarita Mayurvarna Mahavihara
9. U *baha*	Shivadeva Varma Samskarita Sri Rudravarna Unkulinama Mahavihara
10. Guji *baha*	Vaisya Sri Divakaravarma Samskarita Mahavihara.
11. Tanga *baha*	Yampi Balarchana Samskarita Jyesthavarma Mahavihara
12. Chuka *baha*	Mana Deva Samskarita Chakravarna Mahavihara
13. Ta *baha*	Bhuvanakara Varma Samskarita Dharmakirti Mahavihara
14. Dau *baha*	Rudradeva Garga Gotra Varma Samskarita Sri Dattanama Mahavihara
15. Ha *baha*	Sri Laksmi Kalyana Varma Samskarita Ratnakara Mahavihara

The other three additional *Mu baha* include—

1. Cilancho baha — Jagatpala Varma Samskarita Padma Kasthagiri Mahavihara

2. Cho baha — Indradeva Samskarita Sri Asanalokesvara Mahavihara
3. Si baha — Sri Vachha Mahavihara

All the *Viharas* are prototypes of one another. There is not much difference between them. However, slight variations may occur in ritual practices, festival celebrations, and *Guthi* observations, as well as minor planning differences in sacred structures. Basically, there are no major differences, though.

References

1. John K. Locke: *Buddhist Monasteries of Nepal*, Kathmandu: Sahayogi Press, 1985, p. iii.
2. Min Bahadur Shakya, *A Short History of Buddhism in Nepal*, Lalitpur: Y. M. B. A, 1986, p.55
3. Hera Kaji Vajracharya:*Yalaya Bouddha Vihara*, Lalitpur: Bouddha Vihara Sangha, 2057, pp. 5-12; Hem Raj Shakya, *Rudravarna Mahavihara ya Chhagu Adhyayan*, Lalitpur: Buddha Jayanti Samaroha Samiti, 2051 B. S., p. 20.
4. Locke, f .n. no. 1, pp. 3, 21-28, 247 and 425-27.
5. Some Buddhist *Sanghas* in Bhaktapur and Banepa observe only one-day *Barechhoegu* ritual instead of four days common practice.
6. For more information see: Heinz Bechert and Jens-Uwe Hartman, 'Observation On The Reforms of Buddhism in Nepal, *Journal of Nepal Research Center*, Vol. VIII, 1988, p. 1-30; Michel Allen, 'Buddhism Without Monks: The Vajrayana Religion of the Newars of Kathmandu Valley', *South Asia* 2, 1972, pp. 1-4; Stephen Greenwold, 'Monkhood Versus Priesthood In Newar Buddhism', In Fuhrer Haimendorf (ed.), *Contribution to The Anthropology of Nepal,* Warminster: Aris and Philips, 1974, pp. 129-49; Stephen Greenwold, 'The Role of Priest in Newar Society', in James F. Fisher (ed.), *Himalayan Anthropology*, The Hague: Mounton, 1978, pp. 483-503., David N. Gellner, *Monks, Householder and Tantric Priest: Newar Buddhism and Its Hierarchy of Ritual*, New Delhi: Cambridge University Press, 1996, pp. 251-99; Min Bahadur Shakya, 'Historical Analysis of Monasticism In Newar Buddhism', *Voice of History*, Vol. XV, No. 1, June 2000, Kirtipur: pp. 65-80.
7. Indra Kumari Vajracharya: 'Nepalese Buddhist Monasteries:

Aspects of Lakshmi Kalyana Varma Samskarita Ratnakar Mahavihara of Patan', *Voice of History*, Vol. XV, No. 2, 2057 B.S, Kirtipur: pp. 72-74.

8. Dalsha Newami: *Samyak Mahadan Parva Sankshipta Parichaya*, Kathmandu: Dharma Ratna Shakya, 1993, pp. 5-19.
9. Percy Brown: *Picturesque Nepal*, London: Adam and Charles Black, 1912, pp. 63-64. *Also see*: Ranjana Vajracharya: *Role of the Hiranayavarna Mahavihara in Socio-Culture Life of the Buddhist Newars*, (Ph.D. Dissertation submitted to the Faculty of Humanities and Social Sciences, Tribhuvan University), Kathmandu), 2050 B.S, p. 22.
10. Hemraj Shakya: *Maniggal Rajprasad*, Kathmandu: Buddha Jayanti Samaroh Samiti, 2518 Buddha Samvat., p. 4.
11. For details see: Surya Man Vajracharya, 'Lalitpurko Bouddha *Vihar* ra Bouddha Sanskriti', *Rajat Jayanti Vishesangka* ,(Silver Jubilee Souvenir), Lalitpur: Nepal Bouddha *Vihara Sangha*, 2057, pp. 39-41; *Also See*: John K. Locke, *Karunamaya*, Kathmandu: Sahayogi Press, 1980, pp. 32-33; Vajracharya, f. n. no. 3, pp. 4-5; Hera Kaji Vajracharya, *Guita bahi Vihara ya Chhagu Adhyayan,* Lalitpur: Dipawati Pustakalaya, 2056, p. 5.

5

RATNAKAR MAHAVIHARA OF PATAN

The Vajrayana Buddhism of Kathmandu Valley is popularly known as Newar Buddhism. The *Vihara*, therefore, are constructed and operated according to the rules prescribed by the Vajrayana tradition. This version of Nepalese Buddhism is ritualistic and tantric in nature, and emphasizes *Kriya* tantra instead of other tantric practices such as *Charya*, *Yoga* or *Anuttarayoga* practices. However, there are few followers of Nepal's Vajrayana tradition who practice the higher form of tantra.[1]

Ratnakara Mahavihara is one of the fifteen main *Viharas* of Patan. It is an outstanding and well-decorated Buddhist *Vihara* situated at the heart of the city of Patan. This *Vihara* has excellent architectural features as well as artifacts. One of the important features of this *Vihara* is that the *Sangha* members do not dwell on the *Vihara*'s premises, they live outside the sacred structure. The *Vihara* has several names *Ha ba, Ha baha, Hakha baha* and *Hatko baha*, but it is popularly known as *Ha baha* or *Ha ba* among Newar Buddhists. Its Sanskrit name is Shree Lakshmi Kalyana Varma Samskarita Ratnakar Mahavihara, but it has been abbreviated to Ratnakara *Vihara*. This *Vihara* is also known as the *Layeku baha* (the Palace *Vihara*) and the *Kumari baha*. The Vajracharyas of this *Vihara*'s *Sangha* are known as *Rajpurohit* (the royal priests).[2]

History of the Baha

Almost 1100 years ago, there was a Licchivi king named Lakshmi Kamadeva. At that time, there was a place in Patan called *Hwokhu*. There is a very interesting story about the establishment of a *Vihara* on this spot. One night, the king saw a *ratna* (jewel) in *Hwokhu* in his dream. He established a *Vihara* named Shree Lakshmi Kamadeva Samskarita Ratnakar Mahavihara at that spot. It is also noteworthy that a daughter of one of the *Sangha* member established the tradition of *Layaku_Kumari*. The tradition of a living *Kumari* still exists at *Hakha baha*. The present site of the *baha* is different to the original place where *Hatko baha* (*Hakha baha*) was situated. Historians are of the opinion that the original place was the *Lunjhya* (golden window) of Mangal Bazar or the palace of King Siddhi Narsingha Malla. In N.S 740 (A.D. 1620), King Siddhi Narsingha Malla expanded the palace complex. Therefore, the *baha* structure was torn down and then rebuilt at the present site. The reason behind this was to secure a place for the extension of the palace complex. He placed an image of Siddhi Ganesh and Narsingha at the corner and extended the palace complex. These buildings and images still stand at the Patan palace complex.[3]

There are many ideas regarding the original location of *Hakha baha*. The fact that there are *Hakha* and Hauga tole near Patan palace supports the idea that this was the original site, as these places were certainly named after *Hakha baha*. However, there is no other place etymologically named after the *Vihara* which gives further clues as to the original location of the sacred structure. The Newari term *khu* means river. Some other place names are used as suffixes, such as *nyekhu*, *tyekhu*, *balakhu* etc. It is also said that there was a small stream called *Hawkhusi* (river *Ha*) in front of the palace, and that the name of the *Vihara* is related to that river. This fact is further supported by the term *Hakha Chikala* (literally—arrived at *Hawkhusi*) that is uttered collectively during the Matsyendranath chariot festival at Mangal Bazar, when the chariot of the *Bungadyo* (Matsyendranath) reaches the palace area during the *Jatra* (festival). This obviously means that it has reached the *Hakhusi*, but at present, there is no stream. During *Gumla Dharma* in the month of *Shrawan*, a three feet stone image of the Buddha is displayed immersed in water in front of the golden gate of Patan palace complex. The local people worship and venerate the image. The statue, which is displayed at the palace, is said to have originally belonged to *Hatko baha*. This display ritual also proves that the ancient site of the *baha* was within the palace area.

Wright's chronology also mentioned the name of this *baha*. There is a legend that the grandfather of Lakshmi Kamadeva[4] acquired so much wealth with the help of the *Kumari*. Later, he arranged a *puja* for the *Kumari* at Patan palace complex for the first time. He also erected an image of *Kumari*.[5]

John K. Locke has claimed that Lakshmi Kamadeva is known to have ruled from about N.S 135 to 159. He, in fact, succeeded Bhoja Deva. This proves that the *baha* existed some time prior to the reign of King Lakshmi Kamadeva. Another interesting thing to note is the reference of official founding of the cult of the *Kumari* at this *baha*.

No any other evidence has been found so far to support this historical interpretation. This *Vihara* was originally built near the place of the King Siddhi Narsingha Malla. This is accepted date of existence of *Hakha baha*.

The previous name of this *Vihara* was Hatko *baha*. A *tadpatra* related to a land transaction during the medieval period in *Wuku baha* mentioned the selling of a plot of land, whose western boundary, as mentioned in the transaction document, is the plot of Udayapal Varma of *Hatko Vihara*.[6]

Another land deal dated N.S 503 stated that Pradhan Mahapatra Jaya Bir Barman of Hatko *Vihara* was the witness.[7] Similarly, a document of N.S. 505 also refers to Hatko *Vihara*, but it does not give any indication of the site of this *Vihara*. Since then, several *tadpatras* on land transaction have also mentioned the name of this *Vihara*.

In the present *baha* complex, the earliest date mentioned so far is N.S. 776, which is written on a bell from the reign of King Siddhi Narsingha Malla.

Inscriptions of *Hakha* Baha

Since the documentary evidence kept at *Hakha baha* is not accessible to researchers, one is compelled to rely on other inscriptions found in the *Hakha baha* courtyard. In fact, the inaccessibility of those records has had a direct impact on the formation of a historical record of the activities of this *baha*. However, this description attempts to uphold the accuracy of the historical description of the *baha* based on facts derived from other inscriptions.

Inscriptions are of prime importance in the study of history, religion, culture and other aspects of human bahaviour. They always play an important role in establishing facts and putting together a systematic history from scattered evidence.

There are as many as fifteen inscriptions found in the *baha* complex, inscribed on stones as well as metal sheets. Inscriptions are found even around the *Dharmadhatu* and *Vajradhatu Mandalas* in the courtyard. These mainly mention the donor and their devotion to the Buddha. Inscriptions are also found on metal flags, metal repouse above the main entrance of *Kwapadyo.* Independent inscriptions are installed by the side of the *Gandhakuti*, and metal sheet inscriptions installed right below the images of the seven Buddhas in the main building. Furthermore, most of the wooden struts bear some letters inscribed so far which are not readable at present. There are separate stone inscriptions dedicated in the names of *Hakha baha*, *Kumari* and *Vajrasattwa*. The availability of inscriptions helps researchers to analyse the history of the *baha* systematically, and they are of prime importance while conducting research on *Hakha baha*. Some of the inscriptions, which are readable, are included in the appendix section.

There are various opinions on the type of Buddha that was installed as *Kwapadyo* in this *baha*. One group of scholars opines that the *Kwapadyo* is *Akshobhya* whereas other claim it is Shakyamuni Buddha. The inscription states that it is Shakyamuni Buddha. The fact that the main shrine faces north further proves it to be that of Shakyamuni Buddha.

- The oldest inscription found in this *baha* is dated N.S. 793, and describes a donation made by *Upasaka* Gwaniraj Bharo and his wife Bhuvaniju. It is in fragments, however, so most of it is not legible.[8]
- The inscription of N.S. 801 mentions that during the time of *Chakreshvar* Sri Chandra Muni and other *Ajus* Sri Kanakaju, Sri Debaju, Sri Sambhar Debaju, Sri Dharaju, Sri Shikshya Maniju and Sri Dharanju (Chiefs of *Dasaparamita*), Kashi Ram Mulmi paved the courtyard with bricks.[9]
- Another inscription dated 868 N.S. is very important in this research and in the study of the activities of *Hakha baha*. It lists some rules that are to be followed in the *baha*.[10] If one fails to follow the rules, one is supposed to be punished for the *Panchamahapapa* (five kinds of great sins). Some of those rules include—
    1. Eating *baji* (beaten rice) in this *Vihara* is prohibited.
    2. *Mathawangu thasaye bankodae madu*
    3. *Chole phai chi madu*
    4. *Tharapa womhanga sanchhi samohana dhaya yaye madu.*
- The other inscription dated N.S. 959, concerns the renovation of the temple of Shakyamuni Buddha. This was done under the leadership of *Chakresvari Thapaju,* Sri Shiriju, Sri Bhaju Dhan Singhju, Sri Bhaju Dhanju, Sri Bhaju Tadhi Dhanju, Sri Dhanbhaiju, Sri Birnandaju and Sri Bhajumaniju. This inscription is very important because it clearly mentions that the temple is of Shakyamuni Buddha, and has corrected the mistaken belief that the *Kwapadyo* is Akshobhya Buddha.[11]
- Vajracharya Yoga Narsinghju made an inscription in N.S. 981 to commemorate the installation of Vajrasattwa, Basundhara and Manjushri in the *Nairitya kona* of the yard. It is claimed that his entire family created the *dharmacitta* and tried to promote the welfare of all sentient beings. He further established a *Guthi* donating

some *ropanis* of land to conduct *puja, Busadhan* and *Acha Guthi.*[12]

- In N.S. 1000, the temple was renovated and the roof tile was changed. In N.S. 1013 Shakyamuni Buddha of this *baha* was taken to *Lunchhen Nani* at Dathughol Tole for consecration. This ritual of *Chhen danaa* was done under the leadership of Sri *Chakreswore* Thapaju Sri Din Singhju.[13]
- In 1025 N.S, the residential complex of this *baha* was constructed. Some other renovations were also made within two years. All of these constructions and renovations were done in N.S. 1028 when Dhanawanta Singh was the *Chakresvari* and *Thapaju.*[14]
- Again in *Samvat* 1035, Harsha Jyoti Vajracharya, his brothers, sons and wives, covered the outer path of the *Vihara* in the west with stones in order to create the *dharmacitta.*[15]
- In 1054, the main temple was renovated under the leadership of *Sri Chakresvari Thapaju*, Sri Buddiman Ju and other *Ajus.* Construction work was undertaken and deities were installed according to the required religious rituals in N.S.1056.

Kacha Baha

The main monasteries (*Mu baha*) in Patan are organized in such a way that several *Kacha baha* (branch *baha*) are affiliated with them. The *Kacha bahu* may be defined as subordinate *baha*, usually very small in size and with simpler rituals. As a rule, the *barechhoyegu*, the most important initiation ritual among the followers of Vajrayana Newars, is performed only in the main *baha*. The Shakyas perform the ritual in *Kacha baha* also. There are references that state that the ritual is performed in the *Sakha baha* (branch *baha*) as well.

There are one hundred thirty branch monasteries in Patan, which were established by individual *Sangha* members of the main *baha*, *bahi* and *Kacha baha.*[16] In some writings though, it is written that the lay donors built all of the *Kacha baha* in Patan.[17] These are normally smaller than the *Mu baha*, and most of them are modelled after the main monastery. A *Kacha baha* consists of a chaitya, the main shrine of the Buddha, and a tantric room. The tantric shrine is a locked room in one of the adjacent houses, but in some cases, it does not exist.

The main *Vihara* have large number of *Sangha* members, which is ever growing. As a result, it became too difficult to hold the large *Sanghas* together, so, the lay donors were motivated to build *Kacha baha.* Some members could be transferred there to perform all kinds of rituals with the exception of the *barechhoyegu*, and the *Kacha baha* were originally founded this way. The *Mubaha* always provides guidance and support for them.

In general, there are two types of *Kacha baha*:

1. In the first type the *Sangha* members are independent and perform *barechhoegu* independently. The system, according to which they work, is also different from that of the main *Vihara*.
2. In the second type the *Sangha* members are not independent but remain part of the main *Vihara*.

Ratnakar Mahavihara is one of the fifteen *Mahaviharas* of Patan, and has five *Kacha baha* affiliated with it. They are[18]—

1. Dhanvant Singha *baha*
2. Jena *baha*
3. Joga Dhusa *baha*
4. Byasha *baha*, and
5. Byash Raj *baha*

All these *Kacha baha* are located in the vicinity of the main *Vihara*. John K. Locke has provided data about this, but he did not mention Joga Dhusa *baha* and Byash Raj *baha* as the *Kacha baha* which were affiliated with *Hakha baha*.

1. Dhanwant Singha Baha

Dhanwant Singha *baha* is one of the branch *baha* of *Hakha baha*, which is located at Wache Nani tole in Patan. It is also called

Wachen Nani *baha* and it is located just behind *Hakha baha*. There is a small *Chaitya* at the center of the courtyard. The main shrine is that of Akshobhya Buddha, who faces west. There are small images of Ganesh and Mahankal to the right of the shrine. The *Sangha* of this branch *baha* consists of eight households of Vajracharya. They all belong to *Hakha baha*. The *Sangha* of the *baha* is not independent, but is affiliated with *Hakha baha*. There is no tradition of performing rituals such as *Barechhoyegu* and *Achaluegu* in this *baha*. All the *Sangha* members who come within the jurisdiction of the *Kacha baha* perform *nitya puja* and *aarti* every morning and evening respectively. The annual festival of this branch *baha* falls on the full moon day of *Ashwin*. This *baha* has no permanent source of income, so, only *Sangha* families organize the annual festival. There are two inscriptions dated N.S 976 and N.S 1029 on the right and left sides of the shrine in this *Kacha baha*.

2. Jyena Baha

This *baha* is also a *Kacha baha* of *Hakha baha*. It is situated at *Jyena* Baha tole. It is also known as *Sri Jena Nama Vihara*. At present, only the *baha* structure exists. Residential buildings cover three sides of the *baha*, and there are also a Lichhivi style votive chaitya and a stone *Mandala*. On the other side of the *baha*, there are stone images of Narayan and Krishna. The *Sangha* of this *baha* consists of only one household, which belongs to *Hakha baha*. The annual festival of this *baha* also falls on the full moon day of *Ashwin*, and it also has no source of income. According to the local saying, this *baha* predates the transfer of *Hakha baha*. The Lichhivi style votive chaitya probably attests to this fact.

3. Joga Dhusa Baha

This *baha* is also known as Joga Dhusa *Vihara*, and it is situated between *Bu baha* and *Dau baha*. The shrine of this *baha* is dedicated to Akshobhya Buddha and faces east. On the right side of the shrine, there are small stone images of Ganesh and Mahangkal. A small metal bell dated N.S. 972 and an inscription dated N.S 975 are also in the *baha* yard.

At the center of the courtyard, there is a stone votive chaitya right in front of the shrine. *Hakha baha Sangha* members built the main shrine, and the votive *chaitya* was built by a Dau *baha Sangha* members. This is not an independent *baha*, so, *Barechhoyegu* initiation cannot be performed here. This *baha* has no source of income and no annual festival is celebrated there, but the *nitya puja* and *aarti* are regularly offered at the shrine in the morning and evening. This *baha* also has no *Sangha*.

4. Byasha Baha

It is one of *Kacha Baha* of *Hakha baha* located in the Wache Nani tole. It is situated just behind the Wache Nani *baha* (Dhanwant Singh *baha*), and there is a *Pigandya* at the center of the courtyard. The main shrine is one of Akshobhya, which faces north. A stone image of Akshobhya is there, and there is a small stone image of Ganesh and the Mahankal to the right of the shrine. This *baha* consists of three households of Vajracharya of the *Hakha baha Sangha*. As a *Kacha baha* is not authorized to perform *Barechhoyegu* and other Buddhist tantric initiation rituals. This *baha* has no income, so, no annual festival is celebrated. The regular *nitya puja* and *aarti* are offered everyday.

5. Byash Raj Baha

This *Vihara* is situated in between Dau *baha* and Bu *baha*, and is Bheka Raj Vajracharya's family *baha*. Therefore, it is a private *baha* and there are no other families here. In the courtyard of this *baha,* there are two chaityas; one is a stone *Dharmadhatu* chaitya and the other is a stone *Shikharkuta* chaitya. The main shrine is Akshobhya's and faces west. The right side of the shrine is decorated with small images of Ganesh and Mahankal. This *baha* is not mentioned in John K. Locke's list. Surya Man Vajracharya only mentioned the name of this *Kacha baha*. The regular *nitya puja* and *aarti* are performed regularly in this *baha.*

Patan still has several other main and branch *bahas*. The *bahas* are the religious centers of the Buddhists of Patan. Its history remains very important in the religious and cultural activities of the *Sangha* members. The Vajrayana *Viharas* are the source of Buddhist spirituality and ritual practices.

MONASTICISM: TERMINOLOGY AND CONCEPTUAL FRAMEWORK

Various religions exist in the world to regulate cultural lives of people. Many of the religions have provisions of observing monastic practices. The history of monasticism is traced as old as religion itself. All kinds of monasticism and practices are intended for realization of the ultimate truth and renunciation of individual self.

The word monasticism has been derived from the Greek term '*Monos*'. In Latin, it is called '*Monachus*'. The Greek word *Monos* and its entire cognate derived mean one alone or living alone. Therefore, a monastic may be a *Yogi* (hermit), a wandering ascetic or simply who is not cenobite, and thus embraces eremite and peripatetic life styles.[19] Thus, the term indicates to the idea of solitude or isolation. The term itself has become a controversial issue because many of the world ascetics live in cenobite societies.[20] The term indicates to those who live in the society of ascetics renouncing worldly desires and observe celibacy.

The Christian monks were the first ascetics in the religious traditions of the world. They prefer simplicity in lifestyle, living in poverty, observe celibacy, practice mortification, keep fasting, silence and perform prayer for the pursuit of religious life.[21] They were the ascetics who retired in solitary deserts far from the worldly society. Monasticism requires to be understood in terms of asceticism. In fact, it is the denial of all kinds of worldly desires to attain the spiritual goal. The practice of mortification and self denial are the fundamental factors in the evolution of monasticism. In the western religious traditions, the practice of monasticism has been attributed to the Benedictine tradition for its classical nature whereas the base of monasticism has been attributed to the *Vedic* and *Upanishaidic* philosophies in the east.

Monasticism has become central philosophy in Buddhism, but it is influenced by the Hindu monastic philosophies. Monasticism can appropriately be applied to the *Sangha* in Buddhism, monastic order in Christianity, and the *Sadhu-Sanyasi* in Hinduism. None of the religious traditions in the Indian sub-continent mean the term as singie or living alone. The Hindu, Buddhist or the Jaina monastic live alone or in the group set-off from the rest of the societies. The term in Indian, Arabian and Persian languages connotes to the state of poverty, ecstatic state of mind, dress conventions and observing celibacy. The monastics have greater cultural and religious contributions in all civilizations. Similarly, they contributed in the development of the monastic centers as the places of learning. This feature has further played vital role in the continuity of the religious tenets.[22] Similarly, the monastic centers also contributed in transmitting elements of 'Great Tradition' to the laity. Thus, those centers have been the microcosm of the process of civilization. In the contemporary society, Buddhist monasteries also play such roles. Although classical Buddhist scriptures in Pali do not permit monks to preside rituals as an officiating priest, the monks everywhere perform functional role as a priest for the welfare of the lay believers. For instance, the monks in Korean Buddhism also perform rituals as desired by the individual believers although they are expected to practice *Seon* meditation and study scriptures for welfare and salvation of the entire masses. In present times, monks in different Buddhist traditions play the role of ritual performers rather than concentrating in the pursuit of knowledge and attempt to attain Buddhahood. The monks everywhere perform functional role.[23]

The Buddhist order is truly of monks and nuns and not of the priests. People join the monk community only after renouncing the worldly society and follow certain formalities to attain enlightenment. Buddhism prefers monks and nuns to practice religion. However, Buddhist monks in Korea, Japan, Nepal, India, Burma, Thailand and elsewhere perform the function of a priest. Monks perform rituals and preach religious doctrines during the death rituals. The monks perform all kinds of ritual as desired by the laity. They pray for their welfare. A monk priest may be hired to pray for the success, performs inaugural ceremony of a new house, officiate rituals and festivals and so on. Not only limited to it, the monks preach the *Dhamma* on different occasion. It has been a common phenomenon among the *Mahayana* monks. Not only the *Mahayana* monks, but *Hinayana* monks also perform multiple roles such as that of a teacher, a preacher, a priest, a landlord, and so on.[24]

The term monasticism should be defined broadly to cover religious traditions in the world. In the broader sense, the term denotes to the religious institution, ritual and belief system whose agents, members or participants attempt to practice religious acts that are above and beyond those required by the religious teachings or of exceptional individual religious and spiritual leaders in their society. Those spiritual leaders have interpreted radically the tenets that apply to the entire society.[25] Monasticism as an institution is a universal phenomenon, but there is diversity in rules and procedures. The universal characteristic is that a monastic separates him from the rest of the society to be a hermit or an anchorite or to join the society of others who have separated themselves from the world renouncing desires. The monk community intends full-time pursuit of religious life in its most radical and usually most fundamentalist interpretation.[26]

The inspiration for an individual entering into the monastic order is, in fact religious. But there may be some other reasons to renounce the worldly society. The reasons behind may be the interest to discover the ultimate reality, emancipation of the individual self, other limited personal goals, and desire to mitigate social sufferings. The renunciation is generally aimed at salvation, redemption and liberation of sentient beings. However, in present times, the trend in inspiring agents has been changing to some extent. Sometimes, socio-economic or personal reasons may push individuals to renounce the worldly society and enter a monastic order. Therefore, there could be both the pull factors as well as push factors that lead individuals to enter the monastic order. The monastics are also categorized in two types—institutional and hierarchical. The early Christian monastics were institutional monks who were eremite. All other types are either semi-eremite or quasi-eremite. The Hindu *Rishis* (the seers) and the *Jaina Sharmaneras* (ascetics) also belonged to this type. They preferred living alone and observed ascetic codes prescribed by the religious sect to which one belonged. The priestly and non-priestly practitioners belong to the second category of the hierarchical status type. Technically, a monastic is a sacred specialist.[27] An ascetic may lead all kinds of sacredotal acts. Even in the Buddhist tradition, there is the hierarchy of monks, but usually they are considered equal. But seniority in ordination is counted with greater value.

Comparative Monasticism

The practice of monkhood and monasticism was first introduced in the Christian tradition. In fact, it has been the most favoured aspect of Christianity.[28] The term *monachos* is also a Christian creation denoting to solitary, single minded and celibate persons.[29] Many Christian saints were proponent of prayer, celibacy and austerity. Those ascetics were celibate monks or female virgins in the churches. This type of asceticism in Christianity aimed at complete withdrawal from the worldly society. This kind of anchoresis had been the governing factor of early Christian monachism. Later, the cenobitical form of monasticism developed in Christianity. Christian monasticism was characteristic. The cenobite feature attracted the nobility who contributed in building monasteries in different places. Christian monastic tradition laid priority and emphasis on clerical and monastic life. Since the very beginning, monasteries served as the center of learning and also contributed to transmit the elements of the 'great tradition' to the laity. The early Christian monastics were the patrons who mediated between the divine and the human spheres as the impartial judge of earthly conflicts.

The western monastic tradition continued to grow. The Vatican Council has contributed in the continuity of the monastic tradition as lively as it was in the 4th century.[30] The monastic practice in religions other than Christianity may resemble to the Christian monasticism, but there is no any fundamental relationship between them. The practice of poverty, chastity, humility, obedience and mortification are some of the common features of different monastic traditions. The practice of puberty by the early monastic became an essential feature of monasticism in later periods. Similarly, in some of the monastic traditions, monks preferred to survive in self-labour.[31] Celibacy has become an essential feature of monastic practice. The adopted rules of life were same for all who lived together within the monastery dwellings. The laws, in general, were severe to ensure religious practice as a monastic. The practice of bodily mortification was essential in early monasticism. Celibacy, chastity, silence, fasting etc. were parts of bodily mortification. Most of the world religions regarded fasting as one of the essential aspect of religious exercise. In fact, Buddhists, Hindus, Muslim, and Jainas laid emphasis on fasting to accumulate merit.

In Brahmanism and Hinduism, ascetic practices were recognized as the sacred act. They held a common belief that salvation was not possible without renouncing the worldly desires. The ascetics better devoted to attain the highest goal. The early Hindu ascetics were the religious wanderers. It was the ideal feature of Hindu monasticism. Therefore, an ascetic required to remain in a fixed place. It has been the main characteristics of the Indian religious tradition. The Hindu ascetics had spent most of their time in pilgrimage and wandering. A Hindu *Sadhu* (an ascetic) follows those rules even in present times. The life of a Hindu is based on the principle of the four *Ashram* (abode). A man is supposed to proceed to the *Sanyasa Ashram* during the last phase of his life.[32] The Hindus also established the *Math* (Monasteries) for religious recluse. Similar dwellings were later erected for *Yogis* to accommodate their austere practices. This type of act has always been considered an act of merit. There was no caste distinction among the *Sadhus*.[33] There was no any social barrier created so far to enter into the order although Hindu society has been caste conscious. The Hindu ascetics were bound by the vow of poverty, but on the contrary, the *Mathas* where they live were rich. The Hindu monks are called *Yatin*. They lived on alms. They observed strict ascetic codes as prescribed in *Manusmriti* (the memoir of Manu).[34] They also observed *Ahimsa* (non-violence), *Satya* (truthfulness), *Asteya* (refraining from theft), *Brahmacharya* (celibacy) and *Tyaga* (complete casting). Those rules varied, to some extent, among the ascetic groups. The *Mathadhipati* (abbot) had power to instruct his disciples on religious matters. The Hindu ascetics were permitted to keep robes, a begging bowl, a staff, water pot, rosary, strainer, a pair of sandals and cooking utensils.[35] The Jain monastics comparing to the Hindu ascetics, were very definite to observe rules. Regarding the monastic practice, Buddhist and Hindu practices have certain similarities.

The influence of early *Brahminic* traditions did not allow Buddhism to survive in ecclesiastically organized fashion in its homeland. However, Hindus also adopted some of the tenets of Buddhism. In fact, monasticism in Hinduism is the influence of Buddhism. Thus, some of the tenets of Buddhism are assimilated with the Hindu way of life. Although the ascetic practice of the *Rishis* and the *Munis* (the Seers and Saints) during the pre-Buddhist era was a kind of monastic asceticism. During the course of time, *Shankaracharya* and *Ramanuja* in the 8th and 11th centuries contributed to the development of Hindu monasticism. The main duty of a Hindu *Sadhu* has been the practice of *Yoga,* study of canonical literature, begging for alms, teaching religious philosophy and belief to the laity and maintaining of spiritual knowledge. A Hindu monastic has no social obligation, but the society has various obligations towards him.[36] It is the duty of the laity to provide him with subsistence needs so that they could devote themselves in the religious pursuit. At present, there are some ninety monastic orders in Hinduism. The Hindu ascetics follow different monastic codes. Although some of the rules are based on the *Brahminic* values. However, most of the rules have flourished on the anti-*Brahminical* ideals.

Buddhist Monastic Order: The *Sangha*

This Order of the disciples of the Blessed One—namely
From pairs of persons, eight kinds of individuals-is worthy
Of hospitality, is worthy of reverential salutation, is an
Incomparable field of merit to the world.[37]

The *Dharma* makes it clear that *Sangha* order in Buddhism has greater importance. Thus, the monastic order in Buddhism has laid priority on the study of creeds. The *Sangha*, which is one of the *Three Refuge* in Buddhism has been the central focus. The term *Sangha* is derived from Pali which means the order or community of religious practitioners. Literally, it connotes to the group of people living together for the same purpose. It is as important as the *dharma* and the *Buddha*. Although the teachings of the Buddha are an integral part in the Buddhist philosophy, the monastic order has secured prominent place in Buddhism. In fact, the Buddhist movement began not with the body of doctrines but with the formation of a society of aspirants bound by certain rules.[38] The historical Buddha has founded the community of men and women who accepted the corporate life as the best path to attain *Nirvana*.

The Buddhist *Sangha* is composed of four assemblies—of the monks, nuns, lay men and lay women. There has always been a clear distinction between them. Monks and nuns are those who renounce the worldly desires and enter into the monastic order, whereas the lay men believers follow the path living in the worldly societies. The later do not require renouncing the world. Monks and nuns are distinguished from the lay followers in terms of dress conventions and the way of living. They live in the society of monastics and practice meditation and study philosophical treatises.

In East Asian Buddhist tradition, monks and nuns practice meditation known as *Chan, Zen* or *Seon* meditation. It also has some variation due to regionalism in Buddhism. They generally live within the monastery premises and follow prescribed codes, continue study of religion and practice it as a formalized technique of mental concentration in which every detail is exactly regulated.

The irrational questions or meditation themes are important in meditation among the Buddhists in Korea and Japan.[39] The irrational questions which are called *Koan and Hwadu* in Japan and Korea help in the concentration of mind. It has been an important and inseparable part of Buddhist practice. Buddhist traditions in both the countries lay emphasis on mind. The monk practitioners try to solve *Koans* (Kor: *Hwadu;* Ch:*Kung-an*) at the same time study

Mahayana Buddhist *Sutras.*[40] The irrational questions are assigned to the practising monks which obviously leads them to the greater awareness of reality. They may enter the state of Buddhahood using the path. On the contrary, the laity is also believed to attain the goal commuting at first to the paths to the heavens.[41] In fact, the followers of *Mahayana* creed desire to attain omniscience and become the Buddha and devote to the welfare of all the sentient beings.[42]

The *Sangha* originally is a life and a legal system. It is the place to retreat from the miseries of the world. In the beginning, the Buddhist *Sangha* was created to provide favourable conditions for the practitioners. As a general rule, monks in *Sangha* require to live in poverty, chastity and simplicity. The monastic community, since its first inception, is supported by the laity. They provided food, clothing and shelter to them. The support is taken as an act of piety. Although the situation has changed until now, the monks are ordained to live in poverty, and are permitted to keep only a fan, begging bowl, belt, razor, needle, water strainer, a staff, and a toothpick. Various rules were created to regulate their lives to attain the supreme goal by eliminating all kinds of *Kama* (Desire), *Krodha* (anger), *Lobha* (greed) and *Moha* (Illusion). The *Vinayapitaka* mentions about the first monks at the time of the historical Buddha. As a matter of fact, the number of monks tended to increase. Later on, women were also permitted to enter the *Sangha.*[43]

The monastic code and moral precepts were created both for the monks and the nuns. They are expected to observe the code of the *Vinaya*, whereas the lay believers have to keep five precepts. The monastic rules are contained in compendium form in the *Pattimokha* treatise. In the *Theravada* tradition, the monks recite it as the ritual twice a month in the *Sabbath* days.[44] Monks and monasteries formed indispensable foundation of the Buddhist movement, which became a definite living religious reality.[45] During the time of the historical *Buddha,* there were many wandering ascetics in India. The wandering mendicants were organized under a Guru. The ideas and nature of religious attainment, which the Buddha created for his followers, were already familiar to the Indian mendicants. However, the Buddha's creation was distinct to all other wandering mendicants in the sense that it avoided all types of discriminations. Although it very soon became the cenobite institution of Buddhism, it was not the invention of the Buddha. The Buddha and his followers were initially one of the wandering mendicants (*Parivrajaka*). In the Buddhist tradition, renouncement of worldly society is to become free from all types of ties with the social institutions. In the present time the monastic code depicted in the *Vinayapitaka* has become a problem for monks in many Buddhist countries. The Buddhist monks in countries like Korea, Japan, Tibet, Nepal, Burma, Thailand and so on could not keep the rules and precepts faithfully. The monastic Buddhism has witnessed cultural transformation. So, maintenance of original ideals of Buddhist monasticism living in absolute poverty is not viable for the modern monks.[46] The code has lost its essence in modern times, but the monk community still deserves greater respect from the lay society. Some monks are found who try to live according to the rules prescribed in the *Vinayapitaka*.[47] The practice of Buddhism tends to make an aspirant fully self-denying, trained, inoffensive, gentle and continent person. The mandatory rules are to accommodate monks and nuns to live in simplicity. *Suttanipata* also directs the monks to wander like rhinoceros. The early monastics were more like fakirs than monks.[48] The wandering practice of religious mendicants was impracticable during the rainy season. Therefore, they were compelled to break wandering practices during the rainy days. It was incumbent upon them to remain in a definite place. So, they gathered at various rain retreats called the *Vassavasa*, usually situated in nearby villages where they continued their spiritual quest.[49] The historical Buddha also practiced rain retreats alongwith his followers. The practice continued even after his death. It is assumed that in the beginning Buddhist practitioners probably might have built huts where they gathered fortnightly to recite the *patimokha* rules. The laity also participated in such ceremonies. Buddha has permitted his followers to live in five kinds of abodes—the *Viharas*, the *addhyayoga* (golden coloured house), multi-storey buildings, attics and caves.[50] The impulse towards the settled community life developed collective identity. The support provided by the laity for subsistence of the monk community led to decline the practice of wandering mendicancy, which developed more permanent characteristics of monasticism. Thus, the rules of wandering mendicancy have lost its urgency and much of its mandatory character. At present, begging for alms remained only as a ritual. The Buddhist canonical literature mentions that Buddha regarded monastic life as the normative path to attain enlightenment.[51] The monastic order in Buddhism probably originated as a sect within the *Parivrajaka* differing with other sects in recognizing Buddha as their Master and accepting the *Dhamma* as the central philosophy.[52] The quest for spiritual life is quest for freedom which can be achieved only if ego is renounced first. Such a renunciation implies total withdrawal from the organizational fabric of the society. Since man can hardly live like rhinoceros, even the pursuit of religious life required organization though on a different principle. An aspirant enters the new stage of life and is governed by the authority of one's spiritual mentor.[53] The monasteries gradually began elaboration and were established as the center of learning.

So long as Siddhartha Gautama was alive, the *Sangha* was governed by his wisdom as a Platonic state. Since there could not be his successors, it has been governed by the set of rules. *Vinayapitaka* represents his wisdom, which is modified and augmented by collective experience of the *Sangha.* The practice of rain retreat was forsaken later to the permanent monastic settlements of *Vihara.* This transformation was due to some reasons, *firstly*, the followers were able to built certain coherent organizations, and *finally*, the *Upasakas* donated meritorious gifts of land and raised buildings in which the monk community was able to reside permanently. The support of devotees made the monk community able to devote themselves in monastic activities without having worries for material welfare.[54] Once monasteries were erected, the monk community became monastery centered replacing the earlier idea of the *Sangha.*[55] It was the transition from primitive Buddhism to the monastic ideals. This transition had two-fold consequences, *firstly*, the *Sangha* became independent of and different from the wanderer community, and *secondly*, it marked the beginning of the Buddhist coenobium.[56]

The development of monastic order led to the steady growth of Buddhism in ancient India. The efforts of King Ashoka turned it to the full fledged institutional religion with written scriptures, systematic doctrines, a deified Buddha, ethical precepts and large number of powerful supporters.[57] As soon as the great monasteries were developed, it began to attract ascetics and others from different places. The *Sangha* in Buddhism is much reinforced from the fact that Buddhist canonical was largely developed by monks to the concern of monastic life.[58] The *Sangha* in the broader sense consists of four assemblies—*Bhikshu, Bhikshuni, Upasaka* and *Upasika*. The monks are considered Buddhist elite who are the true *Buddhists* in the proper sense of the term.[59] The *Parivrajaka* community or the primitive *Sangha* connoted its meaning in rather broader perspective. Afterwards, it came to be used as the synonym of the monastic order due to strong emphasis on it.[60]

The development of Buddhist monasticism is the result of a gradual process, changing under pressure of its sociological environment and inner principle of evolution. The Indian pattern of monasticism described by the Chinese travellers does not correspond to the exact nature of primitive monasticism discussed in the *Vinaya*.[61]

The *Sangha* or the community of monks and nuns is one of the important aspects of Buddhism. One, who has faith on the *Three Refuge*, has been regarded as a true Buddhist. The Buddhist assembly has grown larger and got impetus throughout the world. The fundamental Buddhism is tantamount to monastic Buddhism. The observance of monastic discipline varies among regional Buddhism. The socio-cultural basis, indigenous, religious beliefs, economy and regionalism have significant impact on the practice of religion. Even in Nepal, some of the Buddhism tenets are assimilated with Hinduism and *vice versa*. This has been the similar case in Chinese, Japanese or Tibetan Buddhism. During Buddha's life time, an aspirant entered the *Sangha* in a rather informal way. The aspirant was formally accepted as a member of the *Sangha*, and then he lived alone and solitary, diligent, vigorous and the master of himself. He attained the supreme culmination of pure conduct through his own comprehension and realization for he rightly passed from life at homes to homelessness.[62]

Monastic order is open to all of them who are free to dispose of himself and do not suffer from impediments of crimes and contagious diseases. Although there is no any class distinction in Buddhism, Buddha himself preferred recruiting monks from among the youths from the nobility who leave home and lead the life of a wandering mendicant.[63] The monks were permitted to leave the order. An aspirant requires to go through with certain stages of tests for final entrance in the *Sangha*. In primitive Buddhism, *Prabajya* ceremony was the only requirement to enter the *Sangha*. After some years of religious training, the entrants were permitted to take the ordination vow. The earlier converts were the *Brahmans*, but Buddhism demolished all barriers of caste and social hierarchy although contemporary society had been highly status conscious.[64] Buddha preached that no accident of birth should hinder a man from entering upon and prosecuting the path that leads to attainment of *Nirvana.*[65] The concept of brotherhood is well understood in the *Sangha.* In the *Theravada* tradition, monks with some years of standing are called *Sthavira* who heads the monastery. The *Upadhyaya* (the Preceptor) and *Acharya* (the Master) are the learned monks. They usually instruct the novices and lead in congregation. The *Sangha* is open to all without any distinction. In fact, it gives an equal opportunity to all to cultivate the path of righteousness. There is no restriction to abandon the life of a monk and return to the worldly society.[66]

The *Sangha* in ancient India became stronger with its increased expansion. Until the destruction of Buddhist monasteries by Muslim invaders, all the Buddhist *Sangha* housed both *Hinayana* and *Mahayana* monks. The *Prattimoksha* rules were binding to the monks and nuns of both the *Yanas.* The rules were first adopted from the *Brahmanical* codes. This was particularly true regarding celibacy and five precepts of conduct.[67]

Mahayana Buddhism in Tibet, China, Korea and Japan is based on one of the *Vinaya* philosophies. There is variation in observing *Vinaya* because it has various sub-types.[68] It is a moral code for the novices. The monks require following one of the *Vinaya* traditions. The Northern Buddhists are the followers of *Mahayana* creed and train the mind.[69] The observance of monastic discipline is intended to control one's defiled and untamed mind, and strengthen the precepts in accordance with its progressive development.[70]

Although some sects of *Mahayana* Buddhism maintain ancient rules, most of them have lost much of its mandatory character. There are 253 rules for monks and nuns. The rules contained in the *Vinaya* are mostly concerned with speech and physical conduct. They, therefore, strive to practice six perfection and four attributes of *Bodhisattva*.[71] The inwardly mental activity is practiced with creation of the *Bodhichitta*. The monks are concerned with the thought of liberating all the sentient beings, for which the *Bodhisattva* postpones his enlightenment. In all cases, *Vinaya* is binding to them. It binds the communities of monks and nuns in an effective bond leading to the life of a homeless. The *Vinaya* laid proper emphasis on the course of action conducive to make progress towards enlightenment.[72] All the monks within the community are informed of the four rules of monastic austerity and four great prohibitions including refrain from sexual intercourse, theft, murder, and false and self interested usurpation of the spiritual perfection. The rules are very much stricter for the nuns. They are considered inferior to the monks.[73] Any kind of violation of prescribed rules results in expulsion from the order. The monastics are expected to work as the member of a corporate body not as an individual.

The establishment of functional hierarchy in monasteries was not permitted in primitive Buddhism. After the death of Buddha, the monk community concentrated in the doctrine alone. Shortly before his death, Buddha instructed the *Sangha*—

> *What does the community expect of me? Never having to direct it or subject it to my teachings, I have no such instructions for the Sangha. I am reaching my end. After my decease, may each of you be your own island, your own refuge; have no other refuge. Acting in this way, you will set yourselves of the summit on the immortals.*[74]

The Nature of Early Buddhist Sangha

Buddha started the *Sangha* as an eremite leader. He did his best to develop it. The practice of rain retreat led to evolve permanent monastic settings. Lateron, various rules were framed on every delinquency to avoid repetition. Of course, Buddha did his best to make the non-believers believing and believers creating staunch belief. The *Vinaya* discusses on the formation of the first group of his disciples.[75] The first converts to Buddhism were *Annata Kondana, Bappa, Bhaddiya, Mahanama* and *Assaji*. The first batch of some sixty disciples was sent out for missionary purposes to different places. During the early days of propagation, the converts were initiated by Buddha himself. The term he pronounced during ordination ceremony was—*etha bhikkhavo ti* or *ehi bhikkhu*. Various restrictions were also imposed in order to avoid unworthy persons getting into the *Sangha.* An aspirant was required to shave head and moustache, put on yellow robes and utter the *Three Refuge*. A formal procedure of ordination was also introduced. An aspirant must sit on his legs and ask for ordination in front of the chapter of ten fully ordained monks. After being ordained as a *Bhikshu,* he had to rely on alms for food, use cloth made out of rags, sleep under tree and take urine medicines, but the rules were relaxed afterwards. The *Sramaneras* were required to follow ten precepts. Four *Parajika* and other rules of *Pratimoksha* were designed for monks who received higher ordination.[76]

The non-Brahmins who desire to enter the *Sangha,* required going through with probation (*Parivasa*) period of four months. Persons with diseases such as—leprosy, dry leprosy, boils, consumption and fits were not permitted to enter the *Sangha.* Similarly, persons in the royal services, thieves, jail breakers, robbers, offenders, debtors, slaves, murderers, nun violators, schist, and hermaphrodites were also prohibited from entering the Buddhist order. The aspirants were ordained in two ways which is called *Prabajya* (the going forth from home to homeless), and *Upasamapada* (the higher ordination). The latter was to be conferred on an aspirant after ten years (lateron reduced to 5 years) of training who could prove qualified to be a member of the *Sangha.*[77] The monks render services to the teacher, become respectful to all the fellow monks and never speak ill of Buddha, *Dhamma* and *Sangha*.

Buddhist monasticism has in this regard shown recurrent, dynamic characteristics atleast in India and neighbouring countries. More austere way of life of a monk or group of monks attracts more lay veneration and charity. It has often happened that a monk settles down to live in a forest cave, to find the cave rapidly equipped by admiring piety.[78]

The function and duty of the *Sangha* is to preserve the philosophical tradition and other features. During the long course of Buddhist history, *Sangha* has contributed to great extent to preserve Buddhism. The monks also realised their function to strive for enlightenment and preserve the doctrine so that others could do likewise.

The monk community intends to attain the spiritual goal which refers to the attainment that a practitioner might achieve during the training of mind.[79] The *Sangha* is categorized into three major types—

– Great *Sangha*	The *Sangha* presided by Buddha is the great *Sangha*.
– Noble *Sangha*	It consisted of monks who have attained the path to enlightenment.
– Conventional *Sangha*	This type of *Sangha* consisted of those who renounced the worldly society but who have yet to identify the path to attain the ultimate goal.[80]

The *Khandaka* has divided *Sangha* into five types—*Chaturvarga Bhikshu Sangha* (comprised of four Bhikshus), the *Panchavarga Bhikshu Sangha*, the *Bisativarga Bhikshu Sangha,* and the *Atireka Bisativarga Bhikshu Sangha.* This division is made on the number of monks admitted in the *Sangha*.[81]

The *Sangha* has duties towards individual good and common good. The monks in the monasteries study the doctrine and in turn teach to the new aspirants. They could lead a contended, honest and energetic life. They also work for the benefit of the laity. The monastic code has become symbol of the purity of the Sangha. The *Hinayana* monks follow 227 sets of rules whereas the *Mahayanists* have more rules in comparison to it. They are prescribed to follow 253 set of monastic rules. The monastic rules were formulated long before *Mahayana* philosophy was developed.[82]

The Newar Buddhist Sangha

All the practitioners who renounce worldly desire and live the life of a homeless wanderer do so to escape sufferings. During Buddha's lifetime, the community of monks and nuns were known as the *Sangha*. The term *Sangha*, which is derived from Pali, refers to an order of religious practitioners. Literally, it means a group of people living together for the same purpose. The *Sangha* order in Buddhism is of greater importance; it is as important as Buddha and the Dharma.[83] It is important to note that the Buddhist movement began not with the body of doctrines but with the formation of a society of aspirants bound by certain specific rules,[84] which are called the *Vinaya*. Gautama Buddha promoted a communal life as the best path. The Buddhist *Sangha* consists of the assemblies of monks, nuns, laymen and lay women. The ascetics are distinguished from lay followers in dress convention and the way of living. They are also bound to follow specific rules. The early monks lived in chastity, poverty and simplicity.[85] However, they were permitted to keep a fan, a begging bowl, belt, razor, needle, water strainer, a staff and a toothpick.[86] In Buddhism, this community of monks is considered to be one of the *Three Jewels*.[87] The Three Jewels are inseparable elements of Buddhism. The *Sangha* at the beginning was founded as a missionary enterprise within few weeks of the enlightenment of Siddhartha Gautam.[88] After attaining enlightenment, he went to Varanasi and first preached the wheel of the Dhamma (the *Dhammachakra pravattana*) to Kaundanya, Bhaddhiya, Vappa, Mahanama and Assaji.[89] They are popularly known as the *panchavargiya Bhikshus*, and were all Brahmins from Kapilvastu. The first *Sangha* consisted of Buddha and his five disciples. Thus, the first Buddhist *Sangha* was formed in India. It is noteworthy that the first *Sangha* itself was comprised of members from Kapilvastu.

The Buddhist *Sangha* is believed to be the oldest monastic order in the world. The *Sangha* formed by Buddha consisted of only sixty members, who were called the founding members of the *Sangha*.[90] The *Bhikshu Sangha* was established in Saranath after the first *Dharmachakra Pravartana* was delivered in 528 A.D.[91]

The term *Sangha* continued to denote the community of Buddhist monks in ancient times. Historically, the *Sangha* was an institution that developed from a group of wandering *Bhikshus* into the stable community that lives in monasteries.[92]

In the case of Buddhism in Nepal, there are several Lichhivi inscriptions found so far in the Kathmandu Valley. Those inscriptions describe the *Bhikshu* and *Bhikshuni Sangha* during that period. It is mentioned in the Chabahil inscription that a donation of land was made by a generous donor for the worship of the *Mahamuni* (Shakyamuni) and for the *Arya Sangha Bauddha Bhikhus*.[93] The Handigaun inscription of Amshuvarma also mentions the *Arya Bhikshu Sangha*,[94] and another Lichhivi inscription from Chapatatole refers to the *Chaturdisa Bhikshuni Sangha*, which was established in the Patan area.[95] The *Sangha* had a high status in the society and played an important role in the construction and maintenance of the *Viharas*. There is another inscription in Musumbahal, which contains the phrase *Bhikshuni Sangha Samarpita pana purana*, and there is another inscription that mentions *Arya Bhikshuni Sangha* in the Bhaktapur— Chyamsingha area.[96] These prove that the *Sangha* played a prominent role in Nepalese Buddhism during medieval times. The *Sangha* of the *Vihara* were also important in strengthening Buddhist tenets and preaching Buddhism to the people. Four types of *Sangha* existed in the Nepalese Vajrayana *Vihara*. Vajrayana has been the dominant sect in Kathmandu Valley since ancient times. The four existing types of *Sangha* are Sakya *Bhikshu Sangha* (*Bandeju*), *Sakha* Sakya *Sangha* (*Sharmni Bandeju*), *Brahmacharya Bhikshu Sangha* (*Bikshu Bandeju*) and *Chailaka Bhikshu Sangha* (*Chibaha Bandeju*).[97] These details are as follows:

1. *Sakya Bhikshu* Sangha

These *Sangha* members are also called Shakyavamsa and *Bandeju*. They are initiated as Buddhist monks in the *Mubaha*.

2. *Sakha Sakya* Sangha

These *Sangha* members were attached to one of the branches of the principal *baha*. Its members were also called *sramanera*.

3. *Brahmacharya Bhikshu* Sangha

These *Sangha* members were Buddhist monks in the *bahi*, so, they were also called *Brahmacharya* Shakya.

4. Chailaka Bhikshu Sangha

These *Sangha* members were initiated as Buddhist monks before a Chaitya but not in *baha* or *bahi*.

Now-a-days, the *Sangha* members do not use these categories for the *Sangha*. The *Shakyas* and *Vajracharyas* usually perform *Barechhoyegu* rituals for four days. This has been a living tradition in the Kathmandu valley, but during King Jayasthiti Malla's reign, Bauddha *Bhikshus* were still categorized as *Shakya Bhikshu*, *Sakha Bhikshu*, *Brahmacharya Bhikshu* and *Chailaka Bhikshu.*[98]

At present, there are three types of *Sanghas* in the Vajrayana tradition of Kathmandu Valley. They are: Vajracharya *Sangha,* Shakya *Sangha* and mixed *Sangha*. The first type of *Vihara Sangha* is exclusively comprised of Vajracharyas. The *Sangha* of *Hakha baha* of Patan (Skt: *Ratnakar Mahavihara*) only has Vajracharya members. The second type of *Sangha* is that of Shakya. The Waku Baha *Sangha* of Patan (Skt: *Rudravarna Mahavihara*) is an example of the Shakya *Sangha*. The third type of *Sangha* is the mixed *Sangha*, which has both Shakya and Vajracharya. Kwa *baha* of Patan (Skt: *Hiranyavarna Mahavihara*) has both Shakya and Vajracharya in the *Sangha*.

RATNAKAR MAHAVIHARA (HAKHA BAHA) SANGHA

When the *baha* was in the present day palace complex of Patan, there were three lineages of *Sangha* members in *Hakha baha.* One of those lineages was Vajracharya and other two were Shakya. After the *baha* moved to the new place by the order of the king, the Vajracharya lineage became so disappointed with the forceful decision that they left the *Hakha baha Sangha* and joined *Bu baha*. Because they left the *Sangha*, King Siddhi Narsimha Malla conferred the lineage of the *Sangha* as Vajracharya upon the remaining two Shakya. The conversion of Shakya into Vajracharya latter resulted in the use of the term *balan Acharya* to denote the *Sangha* of *Hakha baha.* At present, *Hakha baha* has a *Sangha* of two hundred fortyfive members. Of these, eleven live in Kathmandu, five in Kakani, three in Dillibazar, six in Anama Nagar, four in Putali Sadak, two in Naradevi, three in Tyauda and two in Baneshwore. The remaining members of the *Sangha* still live on the premises of the *Hakha baha*. At present, Babukaji Vajracharya is the senior *Sangha* member. In 1974, the *baha* had about 170 initiated male members. With the exception of the single Shakya family that is residing in *Dharan* in the east Terai, all the members are Vajracharya.[99]

In Yashodhara *Vihara* (Bu *baha*) *Sangha* there are four *Kawa* (lineage). The fourth *Kawa* of Yashodhara Mahavihara is said to have migrated from *Hakha baha Sangha* at the time that the *baha* was torn down by the order of King Siddhi Narsimha Malla and moved to the new place. This lineage is called *Rajguru* lineage. The *Rajguru* lineages can marry other lineages in *Bubaha* because they have no blood relations with them.[100] The Vajracharya of this lineage is called *Rajpurohita* (the Royal Priest). They have *Yajaman* (Client or Patron) who can perform the *Karmkanda* rituals (life-cycle ritual). The *Sangha* members of Iba *baha* and Si *baha* are their *Yajman*. They perform the *Barechhoyegu* initiation in the open courtyard in front of *Kwapadyo*. This practice is different to that of other *Sangha* members of *Bu baha*.[101] The Shakya lineage that accepted the

King's decision remained in the *Sangha* and received the *Achaluyegu* initiation. Thus, other Vajracharyas of Patan refer to them as *Balan Acharya* (the Vajracharya conferred by the order of the King). This Vajracharya *Sangha* has no *yajaman* (client or patron) and they do not perform the *Karmakanda* (life-cycle rituals) although they are called the *Rajpurohit* or royal priests.

At present, this *Vihara* has 245 members. Each *Sangha* member has to take turns performing the duties of a *Dyopala* (priest at the shrine). The turns are decided according to the seniority of the *Sangha* membership. The *Dyopala* serves for fifteen days in this *baha*, but most of the *baha* in Patan normally have thirty day turns. Every *Sangha* member has to sleep at the *baha* for four nights to guard it, joining the *Dyopala*. The *Dyopala* performs a *puja* to *Kwapadyo* four times a day. The *puja* is performed in the morning (*nitya puja*) at 8.30 a.m, as a small boy walks round the locality ringing a small bell. In the afternoon service, a hollow log is beaten 108 times, and in the evening service the *aarti* is performed. There are eleven recognized *Aju* (elders) in this *baha Sangha.*[102] The eldest one, who is the seniormost *Aju*, is called *Chakreshwore* or *Thapaju*. He is the head of the *Sangha* and is authorized to preside over the *Sangha's* activities. He has a secure and respectable position conducting rites, rituals and *puja* in the *baha*. The main duties of the *Aju* are to conduct and manage the *barechhoyegu* initiation for the sons of the *Sangha* members and perform *Achaluyegu* (*acharyabhisekha*) for the members themselves. They also arrange the *Dekha abhisekha* (skt: *Dikshya*) for *Sangha* members and their wives, which is a pre-requisite for appointment as an *Aju*. Someone is to be appointed but did not yet have the *Dekha abhisekha.* A special arrangement is made in order to confer the *abhisekha* on him. The *Dekha abhisekha* is very complicated but can be done in any *Vihara*. Also any *Vihara*, that performs *Dekha abhisekha* can permit members from other *Viharas* to join it. Even the Shakya can participate in it.[103] As concerns the *barechhoyegu* initiation, the age of the male children is not fixed. Generally, they are initiated between the ages of six months and 12 years. No age limit has been imposed so far for the *Achaluyegu* and *Dekha abhisekha*. Most of the *Sangha* members are initiated right after marriage, and initiations are performed for both the wive and husband as well.

Hakha baha has an eleven member committee of *nayaka sthavira* (*Aju*), who are the leading members of the *Sangha*. The highest person in the hierarchy is called *Thapa Nayaka*, *Chakreshwore*, or *Thapaju* followed by *Nwokunayaka, dakanayaka*, and eight other *Nayakas*. Each stage of Bodhisattva *bhumi* (stages) and *paramita* (perfection) is assigned to each *Aju* who holds a specific position in the hierarchy. Therefore, an *Aju* does not need to practice *paramita* or Bodhisattva *bhumi* in order to attain a higher level. The death of a senior *Aju* automatically brings about changes in the existing *bhumi* and *paramita*, so, it has merely become a ritual rather than a matter of practice. One does not need to strive to attain the level of *bhumi* and *paramita*.

In the *Sangha*, there is another ritual functionary who is called a *Betaju*, who is an official appointed by the elder (*Chakreshwore*) as the secretary of the *Sangha* committee. He assists the *Chakreshwore* in performing all types of rituals and *puja*.

In ancient times, a *Sangha* member's family could not marry within their own *Vihara*. Now most of the *Viharas* do not follow this rule, such as *bubaha, Kwabaha, Ubaha* and so on, but this rule is strictly followed at *Hakha baha* until now.

Baha Guthi

The term *Guthi* derives from Sanskrit word *gosthi*, which means association. An inscription from the Lichhivi period indicates that *gosthis* were set up for worshipping deities, ensuring the maintenance of irrigation canals and so on. The socio-religious duty of the *Guthi* is one of the fundamental basis of Newar social organization in Nepal.[104]

The *Guthi* is an integral part of Buddhist society, and can be defined as an organization in which members of the *Sangha* perform certain rituals. In general, all *Sangha* members of the *Guthi* get together once a year and a grand feast is always arranged. The economic foundation of most *Guthis* is further strengthened by the land endowment that they have received. One of the members, or a group of members, takes charge of the *Guthi* and assumes overall responsibility. The rules of the *Guthi* are very strict. If a member fails to follow the prescribed rules, he is fined according to the rules of the *Guthi*. In some cases, their membership might also be lost. Several *Guthis* operate in *Hakha baha*, and different types of *Guthis* exist for different purposes. *Sangha Bhojan Guthi*, *Sandepuja Guthi* and *Lainkyabhu Guthi* are major forms of *Guthi*. *Acharya Guthi*, *Bica Guthi* and *Sana Guthi* are other froms of *Guthi*, which operate with in this *Vihara*.[105] All of the *Guthi*'s activities are normally carried out in the winter. These types of *Guthis* are also found in other Buddhist *Viharas*.

Sandepuja Guthi

This is a major *Guthi* of *Hakha baha* which offers feasts for all male children of the *Sangha* members, who have already undergone the rice feeding ceremony within the year. This *Guthi* is very unique. On the first day of the bright half of the month of Marga, the *Sangha* members perform this *feast*. For each feast, there are eight *pala* (four senior *Sangha* members and four junior members) who are responsible for management. The *Ajus* perform the Yogambar *puja*, which is also known as *Digu puja*.

At that time, the *palas* who fail to come to the *Vihara* as assistants of the *Dyopala* to guard the *Vihara* at night are required to pay a fine of hundred Rupees a day, which is called *Dyopadyanmawo*. This amount is spent on the *Guthi*. The *Ajus* supply *Syabaji* (beaten rice) for this feast. A donor called *Tadhidhan* donated a piece of land for this *Guthi* in order to supply *Syabaji*. The other *palas* contribute other foodstuffs, such as meat, wine, vegetables, curd and so on.

Lainkyabhu Guthi

This is a kind of *Bhojan Guthi*. A feast is given to all the members of *Hakha baha Sangha*, which organizes an annual worship at the *agam* of *Hakha baha* for this occasion. The feast that they offer is called *Sangha bhojan*, or *Lainyeky bhu* in Newari.

The *Sangha Bhojan* is organized annually on the Marga Shukla Navami. The *pancha Sthavira Ajus* perform the ritual, which is known as *Nhwooluyegu*, or the bathing ritual of *Kwabhaju* (the main deity). This is followed by a *homa* ritual, which is performed in front of the shrine. After completing the bathing ritual, the eleven *Ajus* perform *Dasami puja* ritual in *Degi* (*agam*) of *Hakha baha*, which is followed by a *puja* at night called *Mucha Khankeygu.*

In the evening, they all participate in the *Sangha bhojan*. The main item at the *Bhojan* is radish. This *Lainktyabhu Guthi* is performed by eleven *Ajus* and their wives, who are called *ajis*, four *bepala* (*Aju's* assistants) and four senior *Sangha* members. At this time, the senior *Sangha* members pay sixteen *paisa* and other *Sangha* members pay one *paisa* to the *Ajus* as a token of respect. *Ajus* manage all the food. Radishes are brought from *dyokyabha*, which is just behind the *baha.* The ten *Ajus* carry radishes from *dyokyabha* on *Marga Shukla Shasthi* (end of November) for this *Guthi*.

Acha (Acharya) Guthi

Acha Guthi is a prominent Newar Buddhist *Guthi*. All the Vajracharya *Vihara* of Kathmandu Valley have this type of *Guthi*, which is called *Acharya Guthi* in Sanskrit. Only *Sangha* members who have already undergone the *Achaluyegu* initiation can participate in it. This rite is also called *Panchabhisheka.*[106]

The members of *Hakha baha Sangha* belong to a common association called the *Acha Guthi*, which meets once a year. During this time, a *puja* is offered to Vajrasattwa by the *Dyopala*, who takes care of the shrine by offering *nitya puja* and *aarti* (offering of lights). The *Acha Guthi* is performed on *Chaitra Krishna Shasthi* (sixth day of the dark half of Chaitra). This *Guthi* is celebrated for three days on fifth, sixth and seventh day of dark half of the month of Chaitra, but Shasthi is considered to be the main day of celebration. All *Acha Guthi* members gather and participate in the *puja* as well as the feast.

There are sixtyfive *Sangha* members to participate in the *Guthi*. This is the number of people in *Hakha baha* who have received the *achaluyegu* initiation. The seniority of members is still of vital importance for the *Guthi* committee. Four members are selected each time as *Guthipala* (turn holder) who organize the *Guthi* and arrange the feast. There are other four *palas*, called

Walapala who support *Guthi* activities. *Wala* refers to a group or individuals whose turn comes next.[107] The *Guthi's* turn is for two years. Each member must serve as a *Walapala* and then assume the responsibility of *pala* next year. An endowment of land was donated by king Yog Narshing Malla to support *Guthi* activities and included the feast in the *Bhadra Krishna Tritiya* (third day of the dark half of Bhadra). The Basundhara *puja* is arranged in the *baha*, and the Vajrasattwa *Busadhan* is celebrated in the *baha* on *Magh Krishna Tritiya* (first week of February). The role of the *Acha Guthipala* is very important at the time of *Busadhan* because he manages the feast during the Basundhara *puja,* which is also called *Gatiladhalan*.

Sana Guthi

In Kathmandu, this *Guthi* is called *Siguthi*. The role of the *Sana Guthi* is important in all Buddhist *Viharas*. There are ninety members in the *Hakha baha Sana Guthi*, but only the head of a family can become a member. This is a lineage *Guthi*, so if a *Guthiyar* dies, the membership transfers to the eldest son of the deceased. If he has no son, it is still the responsibility of the *Guthi* to cremate the bodies of the widows and unmarried daughters of that member. Nonetheless, they cannot participate in *Sana Guthi* activities. If a youngman separates himself from the family, he has to apply to join the *Guthi*. The *Guthi* is celebrated in *Marga Krishna Dvadasi* (first week of November). The *Guthi's* (*Guthipa*) turn comes on the basis of seniority. A committee of four members is formed as the *Guthipala*. It organizes and manages all the responsibility for the feast during the *Guthi* celebration. The other four *Walapala* also help them during the *Guthi* celebration. The rules for becoming *Walapala* and *Pala* are the same as those of *Acha Guthi*.

The *pala*'s responsibility is great compared to that of other *Sangha* members. If somebody dies in the *Guthiyar*'s family, they provide wood and straw for cremation and a cloth to cover the dead body. They also provide bamboo with which to carry the dead body to the river for cremation. Participation in the death procession is mandatory. If one fails to participate in the procession, a fine is imposed.

This *Guthi* has no endowment of land with which to support the activities. The *Guthipala* contributes some money, and additional funds come from donations made by the members or their families.

The *Sana guthi puja* is performed in the *agam kotha* by the *Rajpurohit Kava* of *Bu baha*. Their ancestors were also *Sangha* members of *Hakha baha* when it was in the Patan Palace complex.

Bica Guthi

This is the third type of *Guthi* which is associated with the death ritual, which is called *Sana Guthi* in Kathmandu. This is an optional *Guthi* for those who can afford it. There are only twentyfive *Guthiyars* in *Hakha baha* at present. The feast of this *Guthi* is observed on *Kartik Shukla Dasami* (middle of October), and all the *Guthiyars* perform *puja* in the *agam* and participate in the feast. The *Guthiyars* visit the deceased's family members within four days, and walk in a row when they go to visit such families.

References

1. For details on different tantra see: Thinley Ram Sashani: *Vajrayana Darshan Evam Sadhana*, Sarnath: Central Institute of Higher Tibetan Studies, 1998, pp. 265-84.
2. Hera Kaji Vajracharya: *Yalaya Bauddha Viharaya Samkshipta Parichaya*, Lalitpur: Bauddha *Vihara Sangha*, 2057 B.S., pp. 87-88.
3. For details see: Daniel Wright: *History of Nepal* Translated from Parbatiya, Calcutta: Sushil Gupta, 1958 p. 142; John K. Locke, *Buddhist Monastery of Nepal,* Kathmandu: Sahayogi Press, 1985, p. 234.
4. It is said that Lakshmi Kamadeva was the son of Bhoja Deva who ruled for 22 years.
5. Wright, f. n. no. 3, p. 156-57.
6. Locke, f. n. no. 3, p. 152; *Also see*: Vajracharya, f. n. no. 2, pp. 88.
7. Shankar Man Rajvamshi: *Bhumi Sambandhi Tamsukharu*, Part I, Kathmandu: Rashtriya Abhilekhalaya, 2040, pp. 79-80.
8. For details text see Appendix no. 1.
9. See Appendix no. 2.
10. See Appendix no. 3.

11. See Appendix no. 4.
12. See Appendix no. 5.
13. See Appendix no. 6.
14. See Appendix no. 7.
15. See Appendix no. 8.
16. Ranjana Vajracharya: *Role of the Hiranyavarna Mahavihara in Socio-cultural life of the Buddhist Newars,* (Ph.D. Dissertation submitted to the Faculty of Humanities and Social Sciences, Tribhuvan University, Kathmandu) 2050 B.S, pp 200-01.
17. Ratnakazi Vajracharya and Vijaya Raj Vajracharya: *Yen Deya Vajracharaya Tacha*, Kathmandu: the authors, 2039, pp. 42-49; *Also see*: David N. Gellner, 'The Newar Buddhist Monastery: An Anthropological and Historical Typology', In Neil Gutschow and Michael Allen (ed.), *Heritage Of The Kathmandu Valley,* Proceedings of an International, Conference in Lubeck, June 1985, p. 375.
18. Suryaman Vajracharya, *Ratnakar Mahavihara Sanskshipta Parichaya,* Yala: Dhusa Jayasa V.S 2050, p. 12; *Also see*: Indra *Kumari* Vajracharya, 'Nepalease Buddhist Monasteries: Aspects of Lakshmi Kalyan Varma Sanskarita Ratnakar Mahavihara of Patan', *Voice of History,* Vol. XV, No 2, 2057 V.S. Kirtipur: p.77.
19. Mercia Eliade, (ed.): *The Encyclopaedia of Religion*, Vol. 10, New York: MacMillon Co., p. 35.
20. *The Encyclopaedia Britannica*, Vol. 12, Chicago: Helen Hemingway Benton, 1978, p. 325.
21. James Hastings (ed.), *The Encyclopaedia of Religion and Ethics*, New York: T. and T. Clark, 1981, p. 787.
22. The two traditions—*Little and Great traditions*—are referred in the study of religious anthropology. This concept of 'Little and Great Traditions' has been applied in the study of religious communities and the civilization process. The sacred specialists belong to the Greater community whereas laities are called the 'Little community'. The tradition derived from sacred texts and the customary laws is the Greater Tradition. See for details:—McKim Marriot, 'Little Communities in an Indigenous Civilization', Marriot (ed.), *Village India*, Chicago: The Chicago University Press, 1958, pp. 196-202.
23. Richard Gombrich, 'Introduction to the Buddhist Way', in Heinz Bechert (ed.), *The World of Buddhism*, London: Thames and Hudson, 1984, pp. 14-15.

24. Michael B. Carrithers, 'They Will Be Lords Upon the Island: Buddhism in Sri Lanka', in Bechert (ed.), f. n. no. 23, pp. 133-46.
25. *The Encyclopaedia Britannica. . .* , f. n. no.20, p. 336.
26. *Ibid.*
27. The concept of religious complex and the religious specialists was first introduced by the Chicago School of Anthropologists to study religious tradition in India. The propounders of the concept are Milton Singer and Redfield Robert. Lateron, the Ranchi School of Anthropologists elaborated it and introduced the new concept of Sacred Complex. *See*: L. P. Vidyarthi, M. Jha and B. N. Saraswati, *The Sacred Complex of Kashi*, New Delhi: Popular Publication, 1979; M. Jha, *Aspects of Traditional City of Janakpur*, Patna: Kitab Mahal, 1979.
28. See for reference: Derawas Chetty, *The Desert A City*, Oxford: Oxford University Press, 1966; David Knowles, *The Monastic Order In England*, Cambridge: Cambridge University Press, 1963; Edward C. Butler, *Benedictine Monachism*, Oxford: Oxford University Press, 1966.
29. Eliade, f. n. no. 19, p. 44.
30. The Second Vatican Council met in 1962-65. There was an internal debate on the forms and ideals of monasticism during the meeting.
31. Eliade, f. n. no. 19, p. 49. The Chinese *Ch'an* Master Hya-Kujo, the founder of the Ch'an tradition (Skt: Dhyana, Jap : Zen, Kor: Seon) believed on self-labour. He gave a guiding principle to Zen that—'a day of no working is a day of no eating'. It has become an important guideline for Zen aspirants. Daisez Teitaro Suzuki, *An Introduction to Zen*, New York: Grover Press, 1964, p. 118.
32. Shanker Thapa, 'Monasticism in Korean Buddhism' (Unpublished preliminary research report submitted to the International Cultural Society of Korea), Seoul: 1989, pp. 8-10.
33. For details on Indian Sadhus, wanderers and mendicants, *See*: G.S. Ghuraye, *The Indian Sadhus*, Bombay: Asian Publication, 1964.
34. *Manusmriti* is a Hindu sacred text written in Sanskrit. It deals with the *'Hindu Customary Laws'* as ordained in the Vedic literature. There are some other *Smritis* too, which deal with different aspects of the life of the Hindus,.
35. Hastings, f. n. no. 21, p. 804.
36. *The New Encyclopaedia. . .* , f. n. no.20, p. 340.
37. N. Thera and K. Thera, *The Mirror Of Dhamma*, Colombo: A.B. Gomes Trust, 1975, pp. 21-23 and 67.

38. E.J. Thomas, *History of Buddhist Thought*, New York: Barnes and Noble, 1951, p. 1.
39. Erick Zurcher, *'Beyond the Jade Gate: Buddhism In China, Vietnam and Korea'*, in Bechert *et al* (ed.), f. n. no. 23, pp 208-10.
40. The monks in Korea, Japan and China practice *Hwadu*, *Koan* or *Kung-an*, the irrational questions which force the practitioners to greater awareness. They practice it alongwith practising meditation. For example, the *Koans* in the Korean Buddhist tradition are likely to be—*'The whole world is a single flower.'* A Korean monk Seung Sahn has edited a book of *Koans* from Korean and Chinese Buddhist traditions and Christianity under the same title. 'Korean Zen Taking Root in The West', *Korean News Review*, Vol. 22, No. 14, April 3, 1993, Seoul: pp. 28-30.
41. Etienne Lamotte: *'The Buddha, His teachings and His Sangha'*, in Bechert *et al* (ed.), f. n. no. 23, pp. 53-56.
42. Etienne Lamotte: *'Mahayana Buddhism'*, Bechert *et al* (ed.), f. n. no. 23, pp. 90-91.
43. Rahul Sankrityayan: *Vinayapitaka*, Varanasi: Mahabodhi Sabha, 1935, pp. 75-95.
44. This is a common practice among the *Hinayanists*. Melford E. Spiro: *Buddhism and Society: A Great Tradition and Its Burmese Vicissitudes*, Berkeley: The University of California Press, 1982, p. 292.
45. Edward Conze: *Buddhism: Its Essence and Development*, New York: Harper and Row, 1975, p. 212.
46. Lee Jong Ik, 'Problems of Vinaya to Monks and Nuns in the Modern world', in Lee Sun Keun and Rhi Ki Young (ed.), *Buddhism and Modern World*, Seoul: Dongguk University Press, 1976, pp, 248-52.
47. *Echoes From Mt. Kaya*, Seoul: Lotus Lantern International Buddhist Center, 1988, pp. 53-58.
48. Sukumar Dutt: *Early Buddhist Monachism*, London: Kegan Paul, 1924, pp. 113-14.
49. *Encyclopaedia Britannica. . .* , Vol. 3, f. n. no. 49, p. 391.
50. The *Cullavagga* VI, 1 No. 2, T.W. Rhys Davis and H. Oldenberg (tr.)., Vinaya Texts III, Maxmuller (ed.)., *The Sacred Books of the East*, Vol. XX, New Delhi, Moti Lal Benarasi Dass, 1975, p. 175. Dutt, f. n. no. 48, p. 55.
51. Dutt, f. n. no. 48, p. 55.
52. H.C. Warren: *Buddhism in Translations*, New York: Atheneum, 1963, p. 420.

53. Spiro, f. n. no. 44, p. 281.
54. G.S.P. Mishra: *The Age of Vinaya*, New Delhi: Munshi Ram Manohar Lal, 1972, p. VII.
55. Keneth K.S. Ch'en: *Buddhism: The Light of Asia*, New York: Barren's Educational Series, 1968, p. 99.
56. Joseph M. Kitagawa: *Religions of the East*, Philadelphia: Westminster, n.d., p. 170.
57. Sukumar Dutt: *Buddhist Monks and Monasteries in India*, London: Allen and Unwin, 1962, p. 57.
58. Kitagawa, f. n. no. 58, p. 177.
59. The *Tripitaka* consists of three parts viz. *Vinayapitaka* (The basket of monastic discipline, rules and precepts), the *Abhidhammapitaka* (the basket of doctrinal elaboration) and the *Suttapitaka* (the basket of discourses—the dialogue between the Buddha and his disciples).
60. Conze, f. n. no. 45, p. 54.
61. Kitagawa, f. n. no. 58, p. 167.
62. Dutt, f. n. no. 48, pp. 1-2.
63. Lamotte, f. n. no. 41, p. 54.
64. Sankrityayan, f .n. no. 43, pp. 5-7.
65. This phenomenon is still existent in the south Asian Hindu Society. See for details: Shanker Thapa, 'Caste and Social Domination', *Ancient Nepal*, No. 105, Kathmandu: Department of Archaeology, 1988, pp. 1-5.
66. Hastings, f. n. no. 21, p. 798.
67. Hansmukh D. Sankhalia: *The University of Nalanda*, Madras: B. G. Paul, 1934, p. 32.
68. W. Pachow: A *Comparative Study of Pattimokha*, Shantiniketan: the Sino-Indian Cultural Society, 1955, pp. 60-62.
69. Vinaya is the moral discipline for the monastics. Its tyeps are: *Pali Vinaya, Sravastivada Vinaya, Dharmagupta Vinaya, Mahasanghika Vinaya, Mahisasaka Vinaya* and *Haimavata Vinaya*.
70. Dalai Lama: *Short Essays on Buddhist Thought and Practice*, Dharmashala: Secretariat of H.H. Dalai Lama, 1982, pp. 13-14.
71. *Ibid.*, pp. 1-3.
72. The six perfections are—Charity, Morality, Forbearance, Perseverance, Collectedness, and Wisdom. The four attributes include: Charity according to the needs of the recipient, Courts in speech, to encourage others to practice virtues, and Guiding others in the practice of virtues.

73. Eliade, f. n. no 19, p. 265. The status assigned to the nuns made them dependent on monks.
74. Sankrityayan, f. n. no. 43, pp. 39-70.
75. Lamotte, f. n. no. 41, p. 58.
76. 'The Sutta Bibhanaga' of The Pattimokha', Sankrityayan, f. n. no. 43, pp. 1-70.
77. The Mahavagga (Mahaskandhaka), *Ibid*, pp. 100-10.
78. Richard Gombrich, *'The Evolution of The Sangha'*, in Bechert *et al* (ed), f. n. no. 23, p. 81.
79. Bhikhu Susobhan, *Buddhism At a Glance*, Kathmandu: Anandakuti Trust, 1985, pp. 78-79.
80. *Ibid*., pp. 82-83.
81. *Mahavagga Kahandaka* 9 :29; Sankrityayan, f. n. no. 43, p. 303.
82. Gombrich, f. n. no. 78, pp. 77-89.
83. Shanker Thapa: *Buddhist Monasticism in Theory and Practice*, Kathmandu: Walden Book House, 1995, p.16.
84. Thomas, f. n. no. 38, p. 1.
85. Thapa f. n. no. 83, p.18.
86. *Ibid*, Also see: The *Seeker's Glossary of Buddhism*, New York: Sutra Translation Committee of U.S.A and Canada 1998, p. 530.
87. For further details see: Locke, f. n. no. 3 p. 53.
88. Christmas Humphrey: *Buddhism: An Introduction and Guide*, London: Penguin Books, 1962, p. 132.
89. *Vinayapitaka*, Mahavagga Sutta No 1, 1, 6, p- 80; *Diggha Nikaya* Mahasatipatthana Sutta No 1, pp.195-96.
90. Humphreys, f. n. no. 88.
91. Prakash Vajracharya, *Bauddha Darpan*, Kathmandu: Dharmakirti Prakashan, 1996, p. 1.
92. John K. Locke; *Karunamaya*, Kathmandu: Sahayogi Prakashan, 1980, p. 13.
93. Dhanavajra Vajracharya, *Licchavikalka Abhilekh*, Kathmandu: Institute of Nepal and Asian Studies, 2030 V S., p. 3.
94. *Ibid*, pp. 320-35.
95. *Ibid*, pp. 382-83.
96. *Pasuka*, year 2, Vol. 10, Ashad 2055; *Also see*: Indra Kumari Vajracharya: 'Vajrayani Samaj ma Prachalit Theravadi Parampara' *Ananda Bhumi*, Vol. 1, Year 29, 2058, p. 31.
97. Locke, f. n. no. 3, pp. 21-23, *Also see*: Hem Raj Shakya: *Rudra Varna Mahavihara Chhagu Adhyayan*, Lalitpur: Buddha Jayanti Samaroh Samiti, 2051, B.S., p. 5; Hera Kaji Vajracharya: *Guita*

bahi Vihara Sangha Chhagu Adhyayan, Lalitpur: Dipawati Pustkalaya, 2056 B.S, p. 2.

98. Locke, f.n. no. 92, pp. 21-23.
99. Michael R. Allen, *The Cult Of Kumari Virgin Worship In Nepal*, Kathmandu: Institute of Nepal and Asian Studies, 1975, p. 351.
100. Mahendra Shakya, *Buddhi Raj Vajracharya's Life History,* Lalitpur: Yashodhara Mahavihara Sudhar Samiti, 2058 B.S, p. 4; *Also see*: Hera Kaji Vajracharya, *Yashodhara Mahavihara Sanghaya Chhagu Adhyayan,* Lalitpur: Buddha Jayanti Samaroha Samiti, 2050 B.S, p. 65.
101. Vajracharya, f. n. no. 100, pp. 76-77.
102. For list of *Aju* see: Suryaman Vajracharya: *Ratnakar Mahavihara Sankshipta Parichaya,* Yala: Dhusa Jyasa, V.S. 2050, p. 12.
103. *Ibid*, pp. 22-26.
104. For details on Buddhist Newar *Guthi* see: David N. Gellner, *Monk, Householder and Tantric Priest*, Delhi: Foundation Books, 1996, pp. 231-50.
105. Vajracharya, f. n. no.102, p. 30.
106. John K. Locke, 'Newar Buddhist Initiation Rites', *Contribution to Nepalese Studies*, Vol. 2, No. 2, June 1975, CNAS, p. 12.
107. Gellner; f. n. no. 104, pp. 231-50.

6

RITUALS AND PUJA IN THE VIHARA

Hakha baha is a Vajrayana *baha* in Patan. It observes several regular and occasional *puja* rituals every year. Those *pujas* are performed in the *baha* as part of the annual ritual. Some of the major *puja* rituals are described here.

Daily Ritual

Daily rituals are an important part of the rituals that are performed in Nepalese *Viharas*. The tenure of the *Dyopala* varies from one *Vihara* to other *Vihara*. In *Ta baha* and *Bhinche baha*, *Dyopala*'s turn is for a week, but in other *baha* such as *Bu baha*, *Dau baha* and *Woku baha*, it is for two weeks. But their duty lasts for one month in *Kwa baha* and *Dhum baha*. In *Hakha baha*, the *dyapa* serves for fifteen days beginning Sunday and ending two Sundays later. At *Bu baha* it starts on Tuesday.[1] In *Hakha baha* the *Dyapa's* turn comes every ten years, whereas it's once in a life time at *Kwa baha*.[2] The ritual offered to *Kwapadyo* is most elaborate in larger *Viharas*. In Patan's, *Kwa baha, Bu baha, Woku baha, Guji baha* and *Hakha baha*, the *nitya puja* ritual is performed four times a day, It is observed only twice or thrice a day in other *Viharas*, and once a day in *Kacha baha* only.

The *Dyopala* on duty is selected to perform the following rituals:

Nityapuja : *Nityapuja* is performed in the morning. It is a religious service offered to honour *Kwapadyo*. This daily worship service is performed by the *Dyopala*. During his tenure, a *Dyopala* spends each night in the *baha*.The room assigned to him in *Hakha Baha* is in front of Avalokiteswar *Gumba.* The morning service is performed at 4.30 A.M. in summer and at 5.30 A.M. during winter. The *Dyopala* purifies himself by taking a bath and opens the *Kwapadyo* room before the *puja*. He also cleans the inner part of the *Kwapadyo* shrine. At that time, the senior *Sangha* members gather at the *baha* and sit in a row to the left of the main shrine. They then begin to chant the *Namasangiti* text. The *Dyopala* brings pure water from the *baha*'s tap and other items for worship. Then he washes the *Kwapadyo*'s face. The senior *Sangha* members who sit outside the *Kwapadyo* room ring the bell, which is located outside the main shrine. Then the *Dyopala* shows the metal mirror to *Kwapadyo* and worships, offering *Panchopachara puja*. He also chants *Danabalena.* After this ritual, the *Dyopala* sprinkles holy water on all the attending devotees and beats the *Dharmagandi* (*Gambhasin*) 108 times. At that time, nobody moves from his seat, they just listen to the sound. This ritual is called *Dekhachyakegu* (opening of the god's *puja* ceremony). Most of the *Sangha* families come to offer the *puja* to *Kwapadyo* every morning. On special occasions, such as *Purnima, Ashtami* and *Sanlu* (*Sankranti* > the first day of the month) many devotees come to offer the *puja* in the *baha.*

Majawanegu: Another ritual is performed at 8.30 a.m. A boy under twelve years of age walks round the locality ringing a small bell. The boy is called a *Bapacha* and the ritual is called *Majawanegu.* When he returns to the *baha,* the *Dharmagandi* is beaten. Then the boy waves the *Chamar*, rings the bell and recites verses *Buddham Trailokyanatham....* After this ritual, the *Dyopala* closes the *Kwapadyo* shrine and goes to his home. For the rest of the day, the *Kwapadyo* room remains closed.

Afternoon Service (Swaphothayegu)

At 3 o' clock in the afternoon, the *Dyopala* performs the *swaphothayegu* ritual. He again opens the shrine, and comes out with the *Dharmagandi* and beats it 108 times. After that, he also rings the bell and chants *Buddham Trailokyanatham*.

Evening service (Saunthayegu)

The *Dyopala* comes in the *baha* again at 6 or 7 p.m for the evening ritual. He opens the main shrine and purifies himself by aspirating purified water on his body. Again, a small boy is sent round the locality to ring small bells. When he returns to the *baha* again the *Dharmagandi* is beaten for 108 times. Some senior *Sangha* members come to the *baha* in the evening too and sit in the front yard of the main shrine. They recite devotional songs while the *Dyopala* offers *aarti* (lights), ringing the bell and waving *Chamar* (Yak's tail) to *Kwapadyo*. This ritual is called *Saunthayegu*. After completing this ritual, the *Dyopala* closes the shrine.

Ordinary Buddhists do not know the aim and importance of beating the *Dharmagandi* four times a day as a ritual. In ancient times, however,

- The first beating of the *Dharmagandi* was to wake the monks and prepare them for meditation.
- The second call indicated for the monks to worship Buddha and recite the holy texts.
- The third call was for religious teaching and discussion.
- The fourth call tells monks to practice meditation on impermanence, selflessness, suffering, and the law of dependent origination.

Dega Busadhan: *Dega Busadhan* literally means conservation. It is a Newari vernacular term, which means the anniversary celebration of the shrine of *Kwapadyo*. It is performed on sixth day of the bright half of Ashad (*Ashad Shukla Shasti*). The main purpose of this ritual is to commemorate the establishment of the main shrine.

On this day, all *Aju* and *Betaju* (assistant of *Chakreshwore*) gather in *baha* to perform the *puja* ritual. The *Chakreshwore* and *Betaju* perform the fire ritual (*Yagya*) or *Homa* in front of *Kwapadyo*. They start the *puja* by lighting the sacred fire only when all of the *dana* items are ready. The priest chants *hymns* and offer those items in the burning fire while he performs the fire ritual. All of the *Ajus* participate in it. After this rite, all the participating members proceed to join a feast. There is a *Guthi* which operate the *Dega Busadhan*.

At the time that the *baha* was established, generous donors donated some land for the continuation of the *puja*. Therefore, this *puja* has a fixed income with which to continue operation.

Bahi Dyo Boyegu : The month of Shrawan, also called *Gumla* is a holy month for Buddhists. *Gumla* begins on 25th July and lasts until 23rd August.[3]

According to the lunar calendar, the *Bahi Dyo Boyegu* starts on 10th day of the bright half of Shrawan and lasts until 10th day of the full moon day of Bhadra.[4] *Bahi Dyo Boyegu* is a Newari word that means to exhibit the deities of *Vihara*. Therefore, the exhibition of these deities is called *Bahi Dyo Boyegu*. This is a typical Buddhist festival which is observed in all the *Viharas*. It is, in fact, celebration of the enlightenment of Gautam Buddha. This exhibition in *Hakha baha* starts at the end of July.[5] On this occasion, the *Vihara* and its deities are cleaned. A pair of Dipankar images is also exhibited at this time. One Dipankar image is also regularly sent to *Sri Baccha Vihara* during the *Panchadana* festival. The images are made of wood and bamboo mat (*paulan*) and the heads are made of gold guilted bronze. The image of Dipankar is called *Kuyampaju* in Newari vernacular. It is also called the *Samyak* Buddha. All other images kept in the *Vihara* are also exhibited alongwith images of the Dipankar. The other attraction of *Hakha baha Bahi Dyo Boyegu* was the exhibition of *tunlapau*. It displays the spiritual work of a famous donor (*Danapati*) of *Hakha baha*, Bekha Raj. Now, this *Tunlapau* is in the possession of his descendants. This tradition of exhibiting the *tunlapau* is longer done at this *baha*. Bekha Raj was a member of *Hakha baha Sangha* who did a lot of spiritual work in the *baha* including—

- Donating a gold guilt roof for the temple in N.S 1000.
- Arranged a *Samyak Bhojan* for Guru, Vajracharyas, Sravaka Bhikshus and Chailaka Bhikshus, Arya *Sangha* of Patan. At that time, he also invited King Prithivi Bir Bikram Shah Deva.
- During the festival of *panchadana,* he donated *pindapatra* and other materials to all the Vajracharyas and Sravaka Bhikshus.

- He established a *Dhrama Dhatu Chaitya* in his private *baha* near his house.[6] During this time, he also performed a Chaitya *puja*, visiting all the Chaityas of Kathmandu Valley.

These activities made him very popular among the *Sangha* members in Patan.

Basundhara Puja: Basundhara is a famous Buddhist deity of wealth and long life. She is also regarded as the goddess of wisdom. She is often described in *Sadhanas* as having one face and six arms. In some descriptions, she has three faces. Her six arms hold various attributes. One right hand displays *Varadumudra*, the other holds *Ratnamanjari*, and the third displays *Namaskara* posture. Her three left hands hold *Bhadraghata*, *Dhyanamanjari* and a *wisdom* scripture. She always sits in the *Lalitasan* position.[7] The *puja* offered to her is popularly known as Basundhara *puja,* and is performed in the month of *Ashad* (July) every year. The *Basundhara* fast is locally known as *Gatiladhalan*,[8] and is observed at the *baha* in the presence of *Chakreshwore Aju*, *Ajus betaju* and the *Acha Guthi* turn holders. It is a two-day fast, which is regarded as very significant by *Hakha baha Sangha*. The *puja* is performed in the *baha* where the image of *Basundhara* is located. On the first day of fasting, the *betaju* makes a *Basundhara mandala* perform the *puja*.[9] The *mandala* is made of yellow stone powder (*potachun*) as well as vermillion powder and is decorated with six *kalashas* (water vases), grains and flowers. The *Chakreshwore*, *betaju* and other observers also participate in the worship.

First of all, they worship Buddha, the *Dharma*, and the *Sangha* in the *Mandala* offering flowers, vermilion powder, rice, fruits etc. Then they worship the Basundhara *Mandala*, offering the same articles. During the worship, the priest also tells the story of Basundhara describing her power. On the first day of worship, all the observers wear saffron coloured robes and participate in the ceremony. They eat a simple vegetarian diet after the *puja* and must abstain from eating salt and meat. On the second day, the Basundhara *mandala* is again worshipped.

There is a tradition of offering *puja* to the *Kumari* also. People believe that Basundhara, *Kumari* and Tara are same but are manifested in different forms on this day. All the observers wear red clothes. The worship offered to *Kumari* concludes the fast. Finally, the *Acha Guthipala* of *Hakha baha* has a grand feast inviting all the participating observers.

Panchadana: The term *dana* literally means charity or giving away. In *Mahayana* Buddhism, *dana* is considered to be a virtue that accumulates merit,[10] so, its role is very important in the practice of Buddhism. *Panchadana* refers to the donation of five kinds of cereals to the members of the *Sangha* and others. It consists of unhusked rice, polished rice, lentil seeds, wheat and salt,[11] which are offered during the *Panchadana* ceremony. This ceremony is called *Panjara* in Buddhist society. The term *Panchadana* has no definite meaning, but was taken from the word *Pangaja* or *Punyaja*, which means the sacred rice. The *Pangaja* is a type of *Kheer Bhojan* (porridge) which is given to the *Araya Bhikshu Sangha*. This ceremony is called *Pangjadana* or *Pindajadana*[12]. In Newari, the day is called *Panjashtami*. This ceremony is very famous among Newar Buddhists, most of whom practice *dana* as part of the religious ceremony. On the last week of July (eighth day of the bright half of Shrawan), *Panchadana* is observed in Lalitpur. But in Kathmandu and Bhaktapur, it is celebrated in the month of September (14th day of the dark half of the month of Bhadra). This day is called the *Jugacharc* in Newari.[13] This practice of giving away alms to the *Sangha* is very old. The *Pindapatravadanam* speaks of the merits of charity.[14] Another Buddhist text, *Kapisavadanam*, also mentions the practice of giving alms to Dipankar Buddha.[15] It concludes that the practice of *dana* is important in Buddhism. It is said that *Panchadana* was started at the time of Dipankar Buddha.[16] The images of Dipankar Buddhas of all the *bahas* in Patan are exhibited at a designated place where the devotees can offer alms, but there is no tradition of exhibiting Dipankar Buddha in *bahis*. Only other images of deities are exhibited during *Panchadana*, for example *Guita bahi* exhibits the image of *Guita Nakin*, who is an elderly virgin named Laxmi Thakur who gave an alms bowl to Dipankar Buddha. Similarly, *Yampi Vihara*

(*Yi bahi*) exhibits the image of Sunya Shree Mishra, who established this *Vihara*. Buddhists believe that offering various items as part of a Buddhist ritual will generate merit.

This ceremony is celebrated for two days in *Hakha baha*. On the first day, the *Hakha baha Ajus* worship Dipankar Buddha, offering *Kalasha* (vase), *Sagan*, *Dawpati*, *Gograsa*, *Nhyankasinamu*, *Mahabali* (*Salawadhan*), porridge and unhusked rice. First the *Chakreshwore* worship Dipankar Buddha, then other *Ajus* follow suit. This day is called *Japuja*. After the completion of ritual worship, the *Ajus* offer golden, metal and bronze alms to Dipankar and sit in a row according to seniority. The *panchadana Guthipala* offers them fruit, and then four *bepala* carry two images of Dipankar from the main shrine and the shrine of Vajrasattwa and decorate them with various gold ornaments. Dipankar is then sent to *Sri Baccha Vihara* in a procession. The *Ajus* of *Sri Baccha Vihara* and the *Sangha* members participate in the procession and are accompanied by a band. The *Sri Baccha Vihara Ajus* and *Hakha baha Ajus* worship Dipankar at the main entrance of *Hakha baha*. The *Hakha baha Ajus* act as the patrons of Dipankar, which they then take to *Sri Baccha Vihara* and then perform the *Japuja* ritual there.

On the eighth day of bright half of Shrawan (*Shrawan Shukla Ashtami*) *Panchadana* material is displayed in front of Dipankar, who is kept at the plinth in front of the main shrine (*Kwapaphaley*). Those materials are given away as *dana* to Shakya Bhikshus and Vajracharya Bhikshus on behalf of Dipankar Buddha. Then *Ajus*, wearing ritual garments sit in a row according to seniority, and the *Panchadana* ceremony starts. First, the *Panchadana Guthipala* offers unhusked rice called *jagulpa* to Shakyamuni (main shrine). Then the same thing is offered to *Agam Devata* (Yogambar), Vajrasattwa, Dipankar *Phudyo*, *Pancha Sthavira* and other participating *Sangha* members. During this ceremony, *Kumari* sits on the *Kwapaphale*. The *Sangha* members who do not celebrate separate *Panchadana* in their houses come to offer *dana* to Dipankar, *Kumari*, *Ajus* and other *Sangha* members in the *baha*. Then the *Ajus* visit the homes of the *Sangha* members at their invitation. The latter arrange a separate *Panchadana* at their homes instead of participating at the *baha*. The four *bepala* stay at the *Baha* for the whole day in order to give alms to Shakya *Bandeju* who go there to take alms from other *Viharas*. The *dana* continues until *Phudyo* arrives at the *baha*.

The *Phudyo* is the image of Dipankar that is kept at *Wuku baha* (*Rudravarna Mahavihara*). It is a brass image of Dipankar in a standing position. *Phudyo* is taken around to places where the *dana* ceremony is organized. According to custom, the *daṇa* is concluded only when *Phudyo* receive alms.

When *Phudyo* is taken to *Hakha baha* the *dana Guthi* offers *Jagulpa* and twentyfive other *Panchadana* materials to *Phudyo*. Then the ceremony is concluded. That same night, all the *Sangha* members and *Ajus* of *Hakha baha* go to *Sri Bachha Vihara* to bring Dipankar back. They are given alms of rice in *Sri Baccha Vihara*. This ceremony further supports the relationship between these two *Viharas*. A ritual song (*tuta*) is chanted during Dipankar procession.

While the image of Dipankar approaches the main entrance of *Hakha baha,* a *puja* is offered to welcome it to the *Vihara*. Then Dipankar is taken inside and kept in front of a *Gurumandala* during the performance of the *Piskanluyegu puja*. The *Panchadana* is again offered to Dipankar, which concludes the *Hakha baha Panchadana* ceremony. Then the Dipankar is taken to its room.

The *puja* is still very important in Vajrayana Buddhism. The *puja* at *Viharas* is similar, however there are a few minor variations.

Barechhoyegu: The *Barechhoyegu* is the initiation rite, which is one of the most important Buddhist rituals. The exact origin of this initiation rite is not yet known, but dates back to ancient times. According to *Swayambhu purana*, in the *Tretayuga, Karakuchhanda* Buddha visited Nepal from *Kshemavati Nagar* with his followers. The followers requested for him to be initiated and enter the *Bhikshu Sangha*. It is said that the initiation rites were started in Nepal at this time.[17] All the male members of a particular lineage (*kava*) are attached to the *baha* as members of the *Sangha*. They perform several rites and receive a monastic initiation for four days.[18]

The *Barechhoyegu* rite in Patan differs slightly from the

Buddhist *Vihara* of Kathmandu. Only those initiated within the lineage become members of the *Sangha*. This rite is performed on an auspicious day, and there is no age limit for participation in this ritual. Generally, the male children of *Sangha* members are initiated between the ages of five and seven in a ritual that takes five days. *First,* they offer beetle nuts and money to the *Ajus*. This ritual is called *Goyedan Teyegu.* In Newari culture, beetle nuts (*Goye*) play an important role in announcing a decision to hold a formal ceremony.[19] The boy requests *Thapaju* to confer initiation upon him that he will be able to enter the *Sangha.* This request is made to *Thapaju* offering money, beetle-nuts and other worship material. Then the *Thapaju* accepts the offer and gives his consent for initiation. For this ceremony, the candidate is taken to the *baha* on an auspicious day that has been chosen by the astrologer. He must purify himself by taking a bath and cutting nails. An officiating priest and the *Ajus* of the *Vihara* conduct the ceremony. In this ceremony, the father's sister (*nini*) plays an important role.[20] After the initiation ritual, the boy becomes a *Sangha* member of the *baha.*

One of the *Dyopala's* duties is to regulate the turns of the four night watchmen who guard the *Vihara* and take attendance. If they miss their turn, they are fined one hundred Rupees per night. If any *Sangha* member organizes a feast at their homes and wishes to invite the *Ajus*, they should first inform the *Dyopala*, who passes the invitation on to *Ajus*. He can also participate in the feast.

Achaluyegu: There is another important rite called *Achaluyegu* or *Vajravisheka*. The term *Achaluyegu* is a Newari term, which means the making of the *Acharya* or the Master. In Sanskrit, this rite is popularly known as *Panchabhisheka*, the five consecrations.[21] They include—

Kalasabhisheka	—	(Flask consecration)
Mukutabhisheka	—	(Crown consecration)
Vajrabhisheka	—	(Vajra consecration)
Ghantabhisheka	—	(Bell consecration)
Namabhisheka	—	(Name consecration)

In Newar Buddhism *Kalasha* (the flask with holy water), *Mukuta* (the crown), *Vajra* (thunderbolt) and *Ghanta* (bell) are essential ritual objects.[22] The *Acharya* initiation is only permitted for Vajracharyas, not for Shakyas.

Generally, there is no age limit for this initiation, but according to tradition, most of the *Hakha baha Sangha* members are initiated right after marriage. This initiation is performed in the presence of their wives. A man who is a prospective *Achaluyegu* candidate has to learn *Lasya nritya, Giti* and *pujasewa* from the priest. Then the *Chakreshwore* gives *Panchabhisheka*. After this initiation, he will be the ritual priest and can perform any type of tantric ritual. There are only eighty initiated members in *Hakha baha Sangha*.

After this initiation, one becomes a member of the *Acha Guthi*. His duty is to take turns as the *Dyopala* at the *Vajrasatava* shrine. The turns are decided according to seniority in the *Sangha* membership, and the Vajrasattwa *Dyopala*'s tenure is for one month. One who is selected as the *Dyopala* performs rituals two times a day on a regular basis. As a rule, *puja* is performed in the morning and *aarti* in the evening. Another one of the *Dyopala*'s duties is to regulate the *Acha Guthi*.

Dekha Abhisheka

Dekha is called *Diksha* in Sanskrit. It is a *tantric* initiation. It's full form is *Dasavisekha Dikshya* or *Acharya Diksha*. During this initiation, the priest gives a mantra to the person who takes *Diksha*. The mantra of *Heruka Chakrasamvara, Vajradevi, Hevajra Nairatma, Khadgayogini, Vijesvari, Chandamaharoshana* and others is given during *Dekha* initiation. Usually, the priest at *Dekha Abhisheka* gives sixteen types of mantras. Both husband and wive participate in this initiation. *Dekha* is essential for appointment as an *Aju*. If someone is to be appointed, but did not receive the *Dekha Abhisheka* yet, a special arrangement is later made to confer the *Abhisheka* on him. The *Dekha Abhisheka* process is very complicated one, but can be done in any *Vihara*. Any *Vihara* which conducts the *Dekha Abhisheka* permits members from other *Viharas* to join it including Shakyas. There is no age limit for initiation.

References

1. Information given by Padma Vajracharya of *Bu baha* during the interview.
2. David Gellner: *Monk Householder And Tantric Priest*, Delhi: Foundation Books, 1996, p. 176.
3. Karunakar Vaidya: *Buddhist Tradition and Culture of the Kathmandu Valley*, Lalitpur: Sajha Prakashan, 1986, p. 30.
4. *Ibid.*
5. The date according to the lunar calendar is *Shrawan Shukla Ekadashi.*
6. This *baha* is called *Bekha Raj baha*, which is a Kaccha *baha* of *Hakha baha*.
7. Mahendra Shakya: *Basundhara Devi Ek Adhyayan,* Lalitpur: Lotus Research Center, 2051 B.S., pp. 40-51.
8. Vaidya, f.n. no. 3, p. 122.
9. For Basundhara *Mandala* see: Hera Kazi Vajracharya, *Nepalko Bauddha Dharmama Basundhara Devi,* Lalitpur, Buddhi Raj and Mim Maya Bajracharya, 2058 B.S., pp. 27-28, 38-44 and 50-55.
10. David N. Gellner, *Monk, Householder And Tantric Priest*, Delhi: Foundation Books, 1996, p. 9.
11. Ranjana Vajracharya: *Panchadana Bauddha Parva*, Kathmandu: Shakya Ja, 2000, p. 1.
12. *Ibid*, pp. 1-2.
13. Vaidya, f. n. no. 1, p. 73.
14. *Ibid.*
15. Hem Raj Shakya: *Samyak Mahadan Guthi,* Kathmandu: Jagatdhar Tuladhar, 2036 B.S, p. 9.
16. Vaidya, f. n. no. 1, p. 74.
17. Badri Ratna Vajracharya: *Swayambhu Mahapuran*, Lalitapur: Jog Raj Shakya, N.S. 1116, pp. 27-32; *Also see*: Vaidya, f. n. no. 1, p. 16.
18. Some *Sanghas* in Bhaktapur and Banepa observe only one-day *Barechhoyegu* (monastic initiation) ritual instead of popularly accepted four days ritual.
19. Sumon Kamal Tuladhar: 'Gwaye Da Tayegu: An Initial Ritual of the Samyaka Guthi, *Contribution to Nepalese Studies* Vol. VII, No. 102, CNAS, Dec.- Jan. 1979-80, pp. 47-51.
20. For details of *Barechhoyegu* ritual performed at *Hakha baha see*: Dunda Bahadur Vajracharya, *Purna Bahadur Vajracharya: A Tribute*

To His Life & Work, Patan: Birpurna Pustak Sangrahalaya, 1996, pp. 104-08.

21. John K Locke: 'Newar Buddhist Initiation Rites', *Contribution to Nepalese Studies*, Vol. II, No. 2, June 1975, CANS, p. 14. The process of consecration (*Panchabhisheka*) is elaborately mentioned in the Buddhist classical ritual texts, which are available in the form of manuscripts written in Newari scripts.
22. John K. Locke: *Karunamaya: The Cult of Avalokiteswar Matsyendranath In The Valley of Nepal*, Kathmandu: Sahayogi Press, 1986, pp. 219-20; *Also see*: Locke, f. n. no. 5, pp. 14-19.

7

THE KUMARI TRADITION

Introduction

The worship of *Kumari* as the living goddess is a very old practice in the Kathmandu Valley. The worship of female deities has long played an important role in religious bahaviour.[1] In Hinduism especially, female power is worshipped in the form of deities in the *Shakta* sect. These goddesses have enormous power. There are other female deities who are non-violent and peaceful.[2] Buddhists also worship female deities. *Kumari* alongwith other deities has a prominent place in Nepalese Buddhism. The *Kumari puja* seems to have originated in the Vedic period.[3] Most Buddhists perform the *Agam puja*, in which *Kumari* is also worshipped. This worship is part of the practice tantrism. In the 11th century A.D., Atisa Dipankar came to Nepal.[4] At that time, the tantric system was very popular there. It is said that he also influenced King Lakshmikama Deva. The later established the tradition of living goddess (*Kumari*) and *puja*.[5] *Kumari* was also regarded as the tutelary goddess of the Malla rulers of Patan. Most scholars said that *Kumari* worship in Patan was started by Siddhi Narsimha Malla in the 17th century.[6]

Wright's chronicle states that *Kumari* worship started at the time of Lakshmikama Deva, the King of Kantipur, who reigned from about 1024 to 1040 A. D.[7] John K. Locke says that his grandfather (Gunakamdeva) acquired a great deal of wealth and conquered a vast territory with the help of *Kumari*. It is also said that Lakshmi Kama Deva started worshipping the *Kumari* in Patan. According to *Vamsavalis*, he ascended to the throne around N.S. 149, started the tradition of *Kumari* worship in Patan, and erected a statue of *Kumari*.[8] Legend says that he worshipped the daughter of a *bandya* living in a *Vihara* near Patan palace. Either Gunakamadeva or Lakshmikamadeva is believed to have started the chariot festival of Royal *Kumari* of Kathmandu.

There is an interesting story about the establishment of *Kumari* of Patan. King Sidhi Narasimha Malla of Patan had faith in the *Taleju Bhawani*, which also has a legend. According to it, the King and *Taleju Bhawani* played dice in the *agam* room every night. One night the queen peeped through the keyhole and saw them. She complained to the King about this matter because the goddess was very beautiful. The goddess also found out so she did not come to play again. This worried the King. One night the goddess came to him in a dream and told him that she would come in other form if he wanted to meet, and advised him to establish a living *Kumari*. She would then enter her body. The goddess also demanded that *Kumari* must belong to a lower caste. The King himself looked for such a family and finally he found the *Dhusas*, a branch of the Vajracharya caste whose traditional occupation was to work with gold dust. The *Kumaris* in Kathmandu were selected from the Shakya family.

According to a *chronicle*, Harsimha Deva brought the goddess *Kumari* in the form of *Sriyantra* from Simraungadh to Bhaktapur.[9] At that time, there was only one kingdom in the valley. The colophon of an inscription mentions that the king himself performed the first *Kumari* worship ritual in 1280 A.D. according to the *Kumari puja Vidhana*.[10]

King Ratna Malla, the ruler of Kantipur, built a small *Taleju* temple in 1501 A.D. Mahendra Malla made the three-tiered temple at the present site and Sidhi Narsimha Malla built the Taleju temple in Patan in 1602 A.D. Thus, the *Taleju* cult was established in all the three cities of the valley.

The *Kumari* of Patan

This *Vihara* has the tradition of a living goddess called *Balkumari*. No other *Vihara* in Patan has such a tradition. Her official residence is behind the *Hakha baha* complex, so this *baha* is known as the *Kumari baha* in Patan. It is different from other *Viharas* in Patan, which is why the *Hakha baha* has a prominent place in the cultural life of the people of Patan. Elaborate rituals are still performed on behalf of the *Kumari*. The *Kumari puja* requires several ritual processes, and there are specific rules to select the *Kumari*, who must belong to a family of the *Hakha baha Sangha* lineage. No other families have the right to offer a daughter in the selection process. Those who do not belong to the *Sangha* lineage but have been initiated into this *Sangha* and accepted as *Sangha* members are excluded from it. They are called *Thyakamasta* (adapted children).

The *Kumari* holds a place of higher respect in the group of deities during *Sangha* rituals. The devotees from other *Sanghas* in Patan also visit *Hakha baha* in order to venerate her on different occasions. Her presence is required during *Bungyadya Jatra* (the chariot festival of Matsyendranath or the Bodhisattva of Compassion). She is taken to *Tapukhu*, Lagankhel, Thati, and Jawalakhel during such festivals, and observes the *Bungadyo Jatra* from *Hakha baha* complex. She has to go to the Patan palace complex also to perform rituals. Perhaps it is a continuation of ancient rituals that were observed during Malla rule in Patan. Even during the *baha puja*, she sits by the side of the *Kwapadyo* at *Hakha baha* and receives *puja* from devotees.

The Patan *Kumari* is the Royal *Kumari* who lives at home with other family members. A member of her family, preferably her father, performs *nitya puja* each morning. It takes almost half an hour to offer objects to her as part of the *puja*. Objects such as incense, lights, flowers, grain, fried eggs, meat and rice wine are offered everyday. Sometimes other people also come to perform *nitya puja* at her family's residence. During the *Dasain* festival, most of the *Sangha* members of *Hakha baha* came to perform *puja* to *Kumari*. There are other people who are not members of *Hakha baha Sangha* who also participate in the *puja*. During this time, almost four hundred devotees come to worship *Kumari* everyday and a dozen people came to worship on Saturdays.

The four types of devotees are—[11]

1. The *Sangha* members who participate in the *puja* as part of the ritual.
2. Those who have been suffering from bleeding problems.
3. Government officials who fear demotion, and
4. Those who want to receive *Kumari's* blessings for mundane benefits.

Kumari is a Vajrayana deity. Worshipping her is one of the most important practices of Vajrayana Buddhist culture. *Kumari* is worshipped at different times, and several ritual objects are required to perform the *puja* which includes the Vajra, a *mandala* supported by a base in the shape of a metallic turtle, a vermilion pot (*Sinamo*), *aarti* (to offer lights), a wine container (*patra*), saucer (*thali*), incense stand, light burner (*Sukunda*) etc. The food may include any type of sweets especially *peda*, *jeri* and *swari* along-with beaten rice (*baji*), soybean, meat, fish, ginger and so on.

Selection Procedure

A *Kumari* can continue to be a deity until her first menstruation. When the first blood is seen, the *Guthi* starts searching for a new *Kumari*. The selection of a new *Kumari* is done according to the qualities the incumbent possesses. She must have the following qualities:

1. Daughter of a *Hakha baha Sangha* member.
2. 2.5 to 3 years of age.
3. They should not have any marks on the body such as small-pox marks.
4. They must have no scars or physical disabilities.
5. Must be approved of the astrologer who reads her horoscope.
6. She must still have all of her baby teeth not fallen out.

First, the girls who possess these qualifications participate in the preliminary selection process. Then the priest of Patan *Taleju* presides over the selection ceremony. Then the girl is taken to the *Bada Guruju*, where his wife examines the body of the selected girl. *Lastly*, she makes the final announcement concerning *Kumari*. This is followed by a *Puja* offering incense sticks, flowers, grain, white rice (*akshat*), food and fruit. The selection information is also passed on to the king, and then the *Kumari* is taken back to *Hakha baha*. Worship is also performed at the *baha* complex to mark her selection, which recognizes her as the *Kumari*. The installation ceremony is observed on the *Maha Ashtami* during the *Dasain* festival.

The installation ceremony of the Patan *Kumari* is somewhat different from that of the *Kumari* of Kathmandu, and is called *Kumari Sthapana Puja*. In this selection, the girl sits in front of the priest where she undergoes the purification ceremony. The officiating priest sprinkles holy water to purify her. This is called *angashodhan puja*. The priest purifies each of her six sensitive organs by enchanting *mantra* and making a touch to each part with a bundle of *Kush* (the holy grass), a gray twig tree bark and various kinds of holy leaves. After the ceremony is over, a ritual food comprised of boiled eggs, beaten rice, curd, dried fish, boiled meat and rice-wine is offered to the *Kumari*. She is given red clothes and ornaments. The goddess's ornaments are very important and sacred. She always wears a silver necklace called talisman (*Jantra*) which has a pendant of small right hand conchshell (*Shankha*). In addition to that, other ornaments she wears include chainlike necklace (*Sikrimala*), necklace of severed human heads (*Narmundamala*), a short hollow thick tube (*Tayo*), earrings and bangles. She sits on a throne (low chair) with *Sriyantra* on it. Later, the priest covers the chair with a clean cloth.

At present, the government also provides some allowances to *Kumari* through the *Guthi Sansthan*. The municipality also provides her with a certain amount. The family receives no other financial gains other than the virtue and merit they deserve. The future of *ex-Kumaris* is uncertain, but *Guthi Sansthan* provides a certain amount of money to them too. The officiating *Kumari* is entitled to Rs. 5000 for *bel* marriage and Rs. 10,000 for marriage. Now, ex-Kumaris also receive Rs. 1000 monthly for subsistence. However, most of the surviving *Kumaris*, who are now elderly have not yet been informed of this decision by the government. The present *Kumari* is given a monthly allowance of Rs. 1500.[12]

The *Kumari puja* requires extended rituals and the offering of various items, but the main feature of *Kumari* is that she is present at the *Homa* (five rituals) sacrifice. However, other types of *puja* are also performed. The main items required during the *puja* include red vermilion powder, yellow powder, dark red powder, incense sticks, handmade incense, flowers, beaten rice, a kind of beaten rice (*Syabaji*), butter in a small ceramic cup, honey, cow milk, one Kilogram of polished rice, soyabeans, ginger, red beer, local wine, wicks, twenty pieces of raw thread, a garland tied with a small piece of cloth, beetle, bread, *dechhapa*, twenty pieces of *Goja* (Tib: *Torma*), two bottles of pure water, dried rice, unpolished rice, stone powder and a plate as a worship utensil. The food may include beaten rice two *Mana*, one *Owpa*, *Lago*, *Lapi*, *Pangulu*, *Tatukhota*, *Buba*, one *Khayapi Chayapi,* yogurt, ginger and red bread. All of this food is offered on a plate called *Jyona lapate.*[13]

The *Kumari* is taken out on special occasions. She also goes out for other rituals, but otherwise has to stay at home. The Patan *Kumari* attends the following festivals:

1. The bathing ceremony of Red Matsyendranath of Lagnakhel on the first day of the black half of Chaitra.
2. Red Macchendranath *rathayatra* at Pulchok on the first day of bright half of Baisakh.
3. The day when the chariot goes from Pulchok to *Gabhal* on the fourth day.
4. During the festival of Matsyendranath in *Gabahal* on the fifth day.
5. At Lagankhel shelter house at the time when the chariot of Matsyendranath approaches.
6. The festival of Matsyendranath in Lagankhel.

7. On the day coconuts are scattered from the top of the chariot near *Iti bahal*.
8. On the day when the chariot is pulled from *Iti bahal* to Jawalakhel.
9. On the day of *Bhoto Jatra* of Matsyendranath.
10. On Navami, the ninth day of *Dashain* festival, she goes out for a ritual.
11. During the month of *Gumla* or at the time of *Panchandan*, *Kumari* comes to participate at *Hakha baha*.
12. *Dhanja liya* and on *Mataya.*
13. On the day of *Gatila* (fasting day) in the month of Bhadra, when the goddess is worshipped.
14. On occasional *Baha puja.*

On the ninth night of the *Dashain* festival, which is called *Navami Hakha baha*, a special type of ritual for *Kumari* is celebrated. Eleven children are brought in the *bahal* as the *Kumari gana* (group), which is comprised of nine girls and two boys. The girls are regarded as *Ashtamatrika* (mother goddesses) and *Ugrachandika* and the two boys represent Ganesh and Bhairav. During this ritual, *Kumari* comes and sits on the *Phalecha* (the wooden raised plinth inside the main entrance). The main priest attends the *Puja* ritual for the *Gana* of *Kumari* in the *Kumari* house. After this ritual, the *Gana* go to the Patan palace complex in a procession led by a band which is flanked by *Mahanta* woman. They take care of *Taleju* temple and bring purified water with which to perform the ritual worship of *Taleju*. When the procession reaches the palace's mainyard, the priest and his assistant perform the *Angashodhana puja* for the *Gana* of *Kumari* at the palace entrance. Then the *Gana* is taken to the first floor of the palace, where the *Mulpujari* (the main priest) and his assistants worship the *Gana* in a brief ceremony. They are offered rice fruit, boiled eggs and a variety of meat dishes. After this ceremony, they are also offered a piece of red cloth and some clay toys, such as a stove, two pots, *Kapan* pan and *Potasi*. Sometimes, they are given money instead of such things. Finally, they are taken back in a procession to *Hakha baha*. Then the *Kumari* is taken to the palace complex with the band in a colourful procession. The

Deo Brahamans—the royal priests at the Patan palace complex—perform an elaborate ritual which takes five to six hours. After the *Puja*, *Kumari* is taken back to her parent's house. On the day of *Vijayadashmi, Kumari* grants *Dashain Tika* to the priest, *Taleju* priests (*Taleju Deo Brahamans*) and finally to all those who desire to receive a *Tika*.

A very interesting fact is that the daughters of *Hakha baha Sangha* members do not need to perform *bel* marriage (*Ihi*). The exact reason is not known, but it is assumed that since the girls of *Hakha baha* participate as *Ashtamatrika* and *Ugrachandi* in rituals, they are considered to be deities. As a result, they do not need to undergo such mundane rituals any more. *Hakha baha* has no records pertaining to *Kumari*. No written documents have been revealed so far at the *baha*. Therefore, historical and other details are as yet unknown. The people of Patan believe that Siddhi Narasimha Malla established the tradition of Patan *Kumari*.

A complete list of *Kumaris* is not available, but a partial list is as follows—

Date	*Kumari*
—	Hera Devi
—	Dyalata
	Ratna *Kumari*
1989-1995 B.S.	Chandra *Kumari*
1995-1999 B.S.	Puna Maya
1999-2001 B.S	Nhyuchye Maya
2001-2003 B.S.	Dharma *Kumari*
2003-2006 B.S.	Chandra Devi
2006-2010 B.S.	Indra *Kumari*
2010-2042 B.S.	Dharma *Kumari*
2042-2049 B.S.	Shova
2049-2058 B.S.	Chandra Shila
2058 B.S.–	Chamia

This list of *Kumari* is only a partial list. The documents in the *baha* are unavailable, and it is not possible to obtain the desired data from other sources. This list has been prepared using information received from the family members of ex-*Kumaris*, and may help others who wish to do further research on the theme.

Reference

1. Michael R. Allen: *The Cult of Kumari: Virgin Worship in Nepal*, Kathmandu: Institute of Nepal and Asian Studies, 1975, p. 1.
2. Karunakar Vaidya: *Buddhist Tradition and Cult of the Kathmandu Valley*, Lalitpur: Sajha Prakashan, 1980, p. 202.
3. Allen, f. n. no. 1, p. 1.
4. Rajendra Ram: *History of Buddhism in Nepal*, Patan: Janki Prakashan, 1977, p. 116.
5. Jhon K. Locke: *Buddhist Monasteries of Nepal*, Kathmandu: Sahayogi Press 1985, p. 151.
6. Allen, f. n. no. 1, p. 34.
7. *Ibid*, p. 13.
8. Surya Bikram Gyawali, *Upatyakako Madhyakalin Itihas*, Kathmandu: Royal Nepal Academy, 2019 B.S., p. 18.
9. Allen, f. n. no. 1, p. 15.
10. *Ibid.*, p. 14.
11. Allen, f. n. no. 1, pp. 38-39; Also see: Locke, f. n. no. 5, p. 54.
12. As informed by Guthi Samsthan, Ta *baha*, Patan.
13. Ratna Kaji Bajracharya: *Yendeya Bauddha Puja Kriya Ya Halamjvalam*, Kathmandu: Nepal Buddha Prakashan, N.S. 1100, p. 48.

8

STRUCTURAL CHARACTERISTICS

Architecture

The Nepalese *Viharas* have common architectural features. They are normally closed on all four sides, and are made of brick, wood, tile and stone.[1] The structures, which surround the central square, are on all four sides. A major portion of the building normally consists of living quarters, shrines and places assigned for other religious and cultural purposes. A *Vihara* generally consists of several rooms which have been turned into a dwelling place for Vajracharyas, *Vihara* officers, and a meeting hall.[2] The *Vihara* structure has normally two storeys. The structure of ancient and medieval *Vihara* is not revealed from historical sources, but it has already been proved that walls surrounded *Viharas* in ancient times.[3]

Most of the existing *Viharas* in Nepal are of medieval origin. The names of prominent ancient *Viharas* frequently occur in the literary sources such as Lichhivi inscriptions and Gopalrajvamsavali,[4] but their features are not described. Therefore, we are unable to draw conclusions about ancient *Viharas,* but we assume that some of the features of the original architecture might have been preserved until this day. The *Viharas* are constructed according to Mahayana-Vajrayana traditions and have the following features: [5]

1. A courtyard
2. An open hall
3. A surrounding raised plinth
4. *Gandhakuti*, the main shrine just opposite the main entrance
5. Secret *tantric* room in *Vihara* (*Agam*)
6. Decorated tympanum
7. Only one main entrance
8. Wooden plinths both side of main entrance
9. A votive Chaitya at the center
10. *Dharmadhatu* Chaitya
11. Source of water
12. A fireplace (*Agnikunda*)
13. *Padmapitha.*

These are the basic features of a *Vihara.* In addition to this, every *Vihara* has images of Mahankal, Harati, Ganesh and Hanuman, who are regarded as the protectors of the *Vihara.*[6]

Two big stone lions are usually installed in the Vajrayana *Vihara* on both sides of the doorway.[7] The main shrine of the monastery is normally a freestanding pagoda temple, but in many cases, it is seen as a part of the other surrounding buildings. However, the *Gandhakuti* has distinct physical features; the main shrine is always opposite the main entrance, in most of the *Viharas*, they always have an image of the Buddha in a windowless room on the ground floor usually facing north. There is another room for the tantric deity called *Agam*. The main secret tantric deities are *Chakrasamvar* and his consort *Vajravarhi*. In some *Viharas*, it may be *Heruka* or *Yogamber*. Tantric *puja* is offered to the deity on different occasions.

Location of Ratnakar Mahavihara

At present, there are fifteen main *Viharas* in Patan. Ratnakar Mahavihara is one of them, and is regarded as an important *Vihara*. It is well-decorated, and which is situated at the heart of the city in a place called Gabahal in Lalitpur. It is locally called *Hakha baha* or *Habaha* or *Haba*. The main structure is located above the road, and the main entrance faces north. East of this *Vihara*, there is another *bahi* named *Nyakan bahi*, and there is scared Hindu place called *Agnimath* south of the *Vihara*. The total area of this *baha* is 3-10-2-2 *Ropani* of land. The *baha* structure is built on an area of 93 square feet.

Architecture of Ratnakar Mahavihara

This *Vihara* is constructed of brick, stone and wood. It looks like a fort because there are no windows and only two doors. The three facades of the outer part of the *Vihara* only have small lattice windows on the second floor. The roof of this *Vihara* is paved with tiles known as *Ayenpa* in Newari. The ground floor has one door each on the west and north sides. The main entrance is directly opposite the main shrine (*Kwapadyo*), and the main entrance of the *baha* stands three feet above the main road. Its outer façade is divided into three parts; on the second storey, there is a wooden *Pancha Jhya* (five windows) above the main entrance. There are large and small wooden lattice windows under the tile roof on either side of the entrance. The entire façade and tile roof was renovated in 1983 AD. The following diagram gives some information about structure of Ratnakar Mahavihara.

Icons of Ratnakar Complex

This diagram shows all the details of this *Vihara*, and is very helpful. All the shrines, deities, *Kumari* house etc. are listed below—

1. Main entrance with circular stone tympanum.
2. Stone image of Mahankal, the guardian deity.
3. Stone Dharmadhatu *Mandala*.
4. Mounted upper part of stone Dharmadhatu *Mandala*.
5. *Vajradhatu Mandala* dated N.S 1046.
6. Beautiful stone Shikharkuta Chaitya dated N.S 846.
7. Big Dharmadhatu *Mandala* covered with engraved metal sheet dated N.S.1018.
8. A pair of stone statues of donors decorated with medieval clothes and ornaments.
9. A Lichhivi white washed Chaitya.
10. A stone Dharmadhatu *Mandala* dated N.S.1081.
11. A stone chaitya dated N.S.1081.

12. A place for the *homa* fire.
13. Five-storey rectangular Pagoda style main temple.
14. A big bell dated N.S.776.
15. Stone four armed Manjushree.
16. A stone inscription that mentions the renovation of *Kwapadyo* temple.
17. *Guheshwari* temple behind the *Kwapadyo* shrine.
18. Bhairav temple with symbolic stones.
19. Stone Padamapani *Lokeshwore*, the lineage deity of the *baha Sangha.*
20. Manjushree *pada.*
21. Two storey *Kumari* house.
22. Wooden Padamapani *Lokeshwore* image in a standing position.
23. Stone inscription that mentions the establishment of the shrine of Vajrasattwa, Manjushree and Basundhara Devi.
24. Three stone images of Vajrasattwa, Manjushree and Basundhara Devi.
25. Wooden standing images of Amoghapasa *Lokeshwore*, Padamapani, Tara and Arya Tara.

The main shrine is a five-storey structure in pagoda style. Its roof has different layers. Two floors are covered with tile whereas the top most roofs are guilded. This is the new roof donated by *Yoganarsingh* Vajracharya and Bekha Raj Vajracharya in N.S 1000.[8] Six large wooden struts inscribed with beautiful multi-armed deities support the first roof. The corner struts contain the images of two *Sardulas*. Four decorative struts on each side and four *Sardulas* also support the second roof. Two decorative struts in each side support the top roof. This *Kwapadyo* building collapsed in 1990 V.S. due to a great earthquake. The present building of the main shrine was restored again into its present shape. The entire three-storey wall at the front is decorated with multi-colour square decorative tiles, which are white, green and red.

In terms of architecture, almost all Vajrayana *Viharas* possess three major elements such as the principal deity (*Kwapadyo*), a votive Chaitya, and a tantric room called *Agam.*[9] *Hakha baha* also has the same features. The principal deity of this *Vihara* is Shakyamuni Buddha. The inscription at *Hakha baha* courtyard mentions that the *Kwapadyo* is Shakyamuni Buddha, but some scholars have mistakenly described the main shrine as that of Akshobhya Buddha.[10] Their assumption is based on the posture of the main deity, but Ranjana Vajracharya has indeed identified the *Hakha baha Kwapadyo* as Shakyamuni Buddha. The inscription found in the *baha* also confirms this fact.[11] Three other facades of the *Vihara* have two stories and are covered with tile roofs. The inner north façade is opposite the *Kwapadyo*, which is different comparing to the west and east facades. The north façade contains the arcade of the main entrance, and resembles the *bahi* structure. The three-storey structure adjoins the main shrine (*Gandhakuti*). The woodwork on the doors and the main shrine (to the right of *Kwapadyo*) is spectacular. There is an entrance and a path for circum ambulating the main shrine next to the Manjushree shrine. If we enter this gate, there is another courtyard, which is just behind the main shrine. In this courtyard, there is two-storeyed structure, which is the official residence of *Kumari*. It is also made of brick, wood and stone. The ground floor of *Kumari*'s house is open. The second floor has only one window and a door. In this courtyard, there is an image of *Guheshwari*, Bhairav, Manjushri, Padmapani *Lokeshwore* and other deities. The image of Padmapani *Lokeshwore* is the lineage deity of *Hakha baha Sangha*. Originally, it was located at Phandole, but it has been transferred to the *baha* complex. There is a passage for circum ambulation behind the main shrine. The size of the passage is 6.5ft high and 3ft wide. There are two deities, *Bishwakarma* and *Nyasadyo* inside the passage. There is another entrance for other parts of the *baha* complex at the end of the passage.

Art of Ratnakar Mahavihara

Hakha baha is regarded as a storehouse of art and architecture. This *baha* is known for very nice looking artifacts. It possesses different images and artwork.

Stone Art

The stone tympanum is decorated at the main entrance of the *baha.* There are three-tier stone stairs which approach the main entrance. The entire structure is raised above the main road. Stone lions measuring seven feet in height flank the doorway. The main entrance is decorated with an attractive concave stone tympanum. Vajrasattwa is depicted on the top holding an umbrella (*Chhatra*). The five transcendental Buddhas (*Pancha Mahabuddha*) are depicted with their vehicles (lion, elephant, horse, peacock and *Garuda*) in the tympanum.[12] On the right, there is an image of four handed Padmapani *Lokeshwore*, and a three-faced, eight-handed Vagesvari is depicted on the left. Two stone *Bhikshus* holding *Chwamo* and wearing *Mukut* (crowns) are standing on both sides of the entrance. John K. Locke mistakenly stated that they are *Salabhanjika* figures.[13] There are two images of flying horses, which are 1.5 feet high. This stone tympanum forms an archway instead of a single panel above the door. When we pass through the main entrance, we see raised wooden plinth (*phaleycha*) on both sides. In the right side of the raised plinth, there is a stone *Mahankal.*[14] Every Vajrayana *Vihara* has a statue of *Mahankal* inside the main entrance for protection. *Hakha baha* also has a black stone *Mahankal*. This *Mahankal* is Vajramahankal, and it is also called *Vajrabir Mahankal* in *Hakha baha*. It looks small and disproportionate. The statue is unimpressive and its age is unknown. It may be assumed that it was established during the construction of the *Vihara*. Gods such as *Mahankal* and *Bhairav* are believed to protect the *Vihara.* At the end of the *Phalecha*, a raised plinth surrounds the main yard. The *Vihara* complex was constructed on all sides on this raised platform.

The main shrine stands on a platform two feet heigh. Three stone stairs approach the shrine. To the right side of the main shrine, there is a four-armed stone Manjushree. To its right, there is a gate which enters the *Kumari* house. There is a small courtyard there with many small stone statues, as well as a stone statue of the lineage deity, which is called *Padmapani*. The images of *Guheshwari*, *Bhairav*, Manjushri have also been installed in the shrine.

On the left side of *Kwapadyo,* there are three large stone images of Vajrasattwa, Manjushri and Basundhara Devi. This is the second most important shrine in this *baha.* Yoganarsingh Vajracharya donated these images in N.S. 981[15] alongwith a plot of land with which to operate the *Acharya Guthi.* Vajrasattava is regarded as the most important deity in Vajrayana tradition. Sixty-five members of *Acharya guthi* of *Hakha baha* serve as *Dyopalas.* There is a stone inscription in the right corner of the shrine, which mentions the establishment of the shrines of Vajrasattwa, Manjushree and Basundhara Devi as well as the *Guthi* endowment.

The Nepalese Vajracharyas believe that Vajrasattwa has a higher position than Buddha. He sits on *Padmasana* in a meditative pose but has no special *Mudra.* He holds a Vajra in his right hand and bell (*Ghanta*) in left hand. He is also called *Dharmadhatu.*[16] There is a separate shrine of Vajrasattwa in *Hakha baha,* which is made of black stone. It is 3 ft. high. This image was made exactly according to the description in the Advayavajra Sangraha, but its colour differs from the description in other classical texts. The *Hakha baha* Vajracharyas regard him as *Dharmadhatu.* The *Hakha baha* Vajrasattwa is a single entity. However, in northern countries he is represented in the *yab-yum* form.[17]

Manjushri

The image of Manjushri is one of the most important images of *Hakha baha.* The image is known as Manjukumar, but is popularly called Manjushri. This shrine is combined with that of the Vajrasattwa and Basundhara. *Sadhnamala* has described Manjukumar as having three faces and six hands. His left hands hold the *Prajnaparamita, Uttapala* and a bow, while his right hands holds a sword and an arrow and show *Barada* posture (*Mudra*).[18] The texts also state that the colour of Manjukumar is red, but the image at *Hakha baha* is black. The image of Manjukumar is only of this type in Patan. Classically, Manjukumar should have three faces, but the *Hakha baha* image has only one, which is against the rules of the Manjushri evocation (*Shadanam*). It is not known why two heads are missing.

Basundhara

This is an important image in *Hakha baha*. Her shrine is also combined with the shrines of Vajrasattwa and Manjushri. The goddess Basundhara is the consort of Jambhala. She is one of the most important and most popular female deities in Nepalese Buddhism society. She is believed to bestow wealth and prosperity, like Laxmi in Hinduism.[19] She is described in meditation texts as follows—

> *She has three faces; six arms and sits in the Lalitasan position. Her three right hands hold a rosary, and a jewel and she displays Varadamudra whereas her left hands hold a vase, dhyanmanjari and a scripture. She wears precious ornaments and silk garments.*

The other type of Basundhara is described as having one face and six arms. The text also states that this Basundhara is yellow. But *Hakha baha* Basundhara image is black.

The size of the courtyard is 43 ft 6 inches east to west and 46 feet 6 inches from north to south. The courtyard is paved with stone slabs and contains three stone votive Chaityas, four *Dharmadhatu Mandalas* and a big metal Vajra. Gyanbir Vajracharya a *Sthavir* in this *baha* donated *Dharmadhatu Mandala* in N.S. 1064. Kul Dhana established another *Dharmadhatu Mandala* next to this *Mandala* in N.S. 1060. Its upper part has brass metal mounted on it. At the center, there is a beautiful stone Chaitya dated N.S. 846, which was established by Lakhbir Vajracharya. Next to it, there is a big stone statue of *Dharmadhatu* covered with an engraved metal sheet, which Harkha Raja and Ratna Raj donated. In front of the *Dharmadhatu Mandala*, there are the stone statues of the donors, who are shown in clothes and ornaments.

The white-washed chaitya is one of the most important feature of this *baha*. It is a Lichhivi style chaitya which stands right in front of the main shrine. The *Ajus* claimed that it was established before the *baha* was constructed, but there is no evidence to prove it. This chaitya is flanked by quadruplicate images of *Nagas* raised at the top of the quadrangles of the four pillars. The *Nagas*' heads are raised, just like the *Nagas* of *Guheshwari* temple. Kula Ratna Vajracharya donated the images of the *Nagas*. In front of the white-washed chaitya, there is one stone *Dharmadhatu Mandala* and a stone chaitya, which was donated by Harkha Ratna Vajracharya in N.S. 1081. The *Mandala* and the chaitya on the ground bear inscriptions in Newari. Altogether there are five stone inscriptions in the *baha* complex. Four inscriptions are in the *Kwapadyo* building and the other is in the eastern block of the *baha*.

Repousse Art images

There are several repousse art images in *Hakha baha* complex. There are also beautiful metal banners hanging at both sides of the entrance of the main shrine. It is believed that Buddha used such banners and a ladder to descend from heaven to the earth to bless the devotees. This maintained a link between heaven and earth. Nhuchhye Bir Shakya of *Na baha* (*Padmavati Mahavihara*) donated the banners in 1996 AD.[20]

Above the entrance of the main shrine, there is a gold gilt tympanum, which depicts images of *Shakyamuni, Prajnaparamita* (Dharma) and *Sadakshyari Lokeshwore* which represent the Three Jewels of Buddhism respectively. At the top, there is an image of Vairochana, which Dhanthanku donated in N.S. 1030.

The repousse images of Sariputra and Mahamuadgalyayana, two of Buddha's main disciples are mounted on each side of the main shrine. They are holding a spatula (*silaku*) in their hands. It is said that it represents the *Chaityavadi* sub-set of Mahasanghika. This is a very common feature of Nepalese *Vihara* decoration. *Hakha baha Tuṭa Guthiyar* donated it in N.S. 1030. These repousse art images are the best art pieces of this *baha*. The images are in a standing position and the figures are translucent. The size of the head in proportion to the size of the body makes clear that these images belong to the latter Mall a period.

There are five repousse windows (*Pancha Jhya*) gilt with gold on the first floor of the structure above the shrine. Two smaller windows flank it. Above these windows, a set of seven gold gilt transcendental Buddha images are kept. Mahamuni Vajracharya donated these images in N.S. 1000.

In the courtyard, there are two *Dharmadhatu Mandalas* covered with a bronze sheet. One *Dharmadhatu* is big and is situated at the center of the courtyard, whereas the other is smaller and is near the *Vajradhatu Mandala*.

Bronze Art

There is a bronze *Vajradhatu Mandala* in the courtyard, Trailokya Muni donated in N.S. 1046. The top second roof of the shrine has three-miniature brass Chaityas in the form of a pinnacle. Purna Bahadur Vajracharya donated these Chaityas. At that time, he was the *Chakreshwore* in *Hakha baha*. There are two large brass lions mounted on the stone base, which are supported by crouching elephants at the entrance of the main shrine. The lions and elephants protect the shrine. Two images of the Bodhisattva, riding lions, are also installed there. Purna Bahadur donated them in N.S. 1058 in memory of his parents Laxmi Jyoti and Astamaya Vajracharya. There is also a metal fireplace (*Agnikunda*) and a *mandala* in front of the main shrine, which were dedicated by Harkha Bir and his wife in N.S. 1000. On the right side of the main shrine, there is a big bell, which was installed in N.S. 776. There is also a metal image of the Hindu god Krishna, which was donated by Tulsi Mehar *Guthi* and is kept in the shrine of *Lokeshwore*. On the day of *Krishnastami* during the month of *Bhadra*, a religious (*puja*) ceremony is regularly organised on behalf of Lord Krishna. Thus, this Hindu god is also worshipped in this *Vihara*, which is a typical example of religious tolerance in Nepal.

Wood Art

This *Vihara* has very nice woodwork. In the eastern and western buildings, there are several wooden decorative windows, and wooden images of Amoghpasa *Lokeshwore*, Padmapani Tara and Arya Tara have been installed in the western building. The images face south, and all are in the standing position. Amoghapasa *Lokeshwore* is white and has eight hands. Padmapani and Arya Tara are yellow and green in colour with four and two arms respectively.

Amoghpasa *Lokeshwore* is a multiarmed form of *Avalokiteshwore*. Amoghpasa is popular not only in Nepal, but in all countries where *Mahayana* Buddhism has become popular. Images of Amoghpasa are found in Java, China and Japan.[21] Amoghpasa has one face and wears saffron clothes. He has eight hands, and his right hands hold goad, noose (*pasa*) and shows

Abhaya Mudra (gesture of fearlessness), while his left hands hold a trident, a scripture, white lotus and a water pot. The image of Amoghpasa *Lokeshwore* in *Hakha baha* corresponds to this description, but its face is white.

This *baha* has a separate shrine for Arya Tara. She is said to be the *Prajna* of Amoghsiddhi and the embodiment of air, so she is green. She is also called the nature of jealousy (*Irsyarati*). It is mentioned in the *Advayavajra Sangraha* that she originated from the seed syllable *Tam* of golden green colour. Her symbol is a light green lotus (*Utpala*), and she has many forms. Her most common forms have two, six and eight arms. The Arya Tara image in *Hakha baha* has two hands and is in a standing position.

There is another image of Padmapani *Lokeshwore* at the left side of the main shrine. This image is said to be older than the image of *Rato Machindranath* (*Bungadyo*), but there is no evidence to support this view. Padmapani *Lokeshwore* is a form of Avlokiteshwore who holds a Lotus flower in his left hand and shows *Varada mudra* with his right hand. In the Kathmandu valley, there are numerous images of Padmapani *Lokeshwore*.[22] In *Hakha baha,* there are two of them. One is the lineage deity of *Hakha baha Sangha*, which is made of stone, and the other image is red and is made of wood.

The shrine of Padmapani *Lokeshwore* surmounted by a small painted wooden tympanum which depicts the images of Buddha (Shakyamuni), the Dharma (*Prajnaparamita*) and the *Sangha* (Padmapani Lokeshwore). There are four well-decorated wooden tympanums in the *Kwapadyo* building. Similarly, three tympanums are in the shrines of Vajrasattwa, Manjushree and Basundhara. These tympanums are made of wooden slabs inscribed with the images of several Vajrayana deities. There are twenty-six wooden struts and ten decorative *Sardulas* that support the roofs in the main shrine. Multi-armed deities, Buddhas and *Lokeshwore* are depicted on those struts, which are very artistic and spectacular.

There are two images of Dipankar inside the Vajrasattwa shrine. Dipankar is made of wood and bamboo sticks (*Paulan*). The head of the image is made of bronze. Dipankar image is exhibited during *Panchadana*, *Gumla* and at the five yearly Patan *Samyak* festivals.

References

1. *Also see*: Ronald M. Bernier: 'Notes on *Chusya Bahal* in Kathmandu', *Kailash*, Vol. VI, No. 4, 1978, p. 233.
2. Sushila Pradhan: *Buddhism in Ancient Nepal* (Ph.D. Dissertation submitted to the Faculty of Humanities and Social Sciences), Tribhubhan University, Kathmandu: 1984, pp. 215-16.
3. Yagbahal inscription of Narendra Deva dated 679 A.D. Quoted from Dhanavajra Vajracharya, *Lichhavikalin Abhilekha*, Kathmandu: CNAS, 2030, p. 505.
4. Dhanavajra Vajracharya and K.P Malla (ed.): *The Gopalrajvamsavali*, Kathmandu: Nepal Research Center, 1985, pp. 76-78; *Also see*: Dhanavajra Vajracharya f.n. no. 3, pp. 320-25, 370-71, 387-88, and 496-510.
5. Sudarshan Bhikshu: *Nepali Vihara Ka Vishesataharu*, Lalitpur: Sradaluharu, 2041, p. 1.
6. Dilli Raman Regmi: *Medieval Nepal*, Calcutta: K.L. Mukhopadhyaya, 1965, p. 864.
7. Karel Rijik Van Kooij: 'The Iconography of the Buddhist Wood Carving'. *Journal of Nepal Research Center*, Vol. I, Kathmandu: 1997, p. 40.
8. Surya Man Vajracharya, *Ratnakar Mahavihara Ya Sankshipta Parichaya*, Yala: Dhusa Jyasa, B.S. 2053, p. 7.
9. David N. Gellner: 'The Newar Buddhist Monastery—An Anthropological and Historical Typology', in Neil Gutschow and Micheal Allen (ed.),*Heritage of Kathmandu Valley Proceedings of an International Conference in Lubek*, June 1985, p. 371.
10. John K. Locke: *Buddhist Monastery of Nepal*, Kathmandu: Sahayogi Press, 1985, p.184; Hera Kaji Vajracharya: *Yalaya Bauddha Vihara Sankshipta Parichaya*, Lalitpur: Bauddha *Vihara Sangha*, 2057 B.S pp. 85-86; *Also see*: Vajracharya, f. n. no. 8, pp. 2-5.
11. Rajana Vajracharya: '*Role of the Hiranayavarna Mahavihara in Socio-cultural Life of the Buddhist Newars*' (Ph.D. Dissertation submitted to the Faculty of Humanities and Social Sciences, Tribhuvan University), Kathmandu: 2050 B.S., p. 22; *Also see*: The *Hakha baha* inscriptions in the appendix which mention Samvat

959 (N.S.) ... Ratnakar Mahavihara ya Sri 3 Shakyamuni Buddha Bhagawanya devar jirnodhar yanga dina juro" (The day on which the temple of Shakyamuni Buddha is renovated and consecrated) - *Samvat 1000 (N.S.) Sri 3 Lakshmi Kalyana Varma Sanskarita Ratnakara Mahavihara Sa Virajita Sri 3 Shakyamuni Bhagawanya Yanga dina juro" (The tiles of the roof of Lakshmi Kalyana Varma Samskarita Ratnakara Mahavihara of Shakyamuni Buddha is dismantled and renovated); Also see*: Vajracharya, f. n. no. 8, pp. 4-5.

12. An interview with Aju Suryaman Vajracharya of *Hakha Baha. Garuda* is mythological bird in Hinduism and Buddhism.
13. Locke, f. n. no. 10, p. 148.
14. Mahankal is also called Vajra Bhairav in Vajrayana Buddhism.
15. Inscription dated 981 N.S. of Hakha *baha* see appendix no. 5.
16. Benoytosh Bhattacharya: *The Indian Buddhist Iconography,* Calcutta: K. L. Mukhopadhyaya, 1968, pp. 74-75.
17. *Ibid.*, p. 75.
18. Benoytosh Bhattacharya, *Sadhnamala,* Vol. I, Baroda: Oriental Institute, 1968, p. 151.
19. Min Bahadur Shakya, *The Iconography of Nepalese Buddhism,* Kathmandu: Handicraft Association of Nepal, 1994, p. 42; *Also see*; Mahendra Shakya, *Basundhara Devi Ek Adhyayan,* Lalitpur: Lotus Research Center, 2051 B.S., pp. 40-51.
20. *Nabaha* is a *Kacha baha* of Yashodhara Mahavihara (*Bu baha*) of Patan.
21. Shakya, f. n. no. 19, pp. 32-33.
22. *Ibid.*

9

CONCLUSION

Viharas have always played a significant role in Buddhists' religious life. In ancient times, Patan used to be a famous and prominent city in the valley of Kathmandu. It is predominantly Buddhist. Many prominent *Viharas* were established in and around Patan in ancient times. At present, there are 167 *Viharas* in Patan. Fifteen of these are considered to be main *Viharas*, called *Mahaviharas*, and twentyfive are *bahi Vihara*. The remaining *Viharas* are called *Kacha Baha*. In addition to this, some *Viharas* are privately operated by individual families, but a common feature is that all of the *Viharas* are prototype of each other.

An inscription form of ancient Nepal records the existence of Vajrayana Buddhism during the Lichhivi period.[1] In Nepal, Vajrayana Buddhism underwent several changes during and after the time of King Jayasthiti Malla. Now, it focuses on ritual practices. So Nepali Vajrayana followers mainly practice the *Kriya* tantra, which emphasizes outward activities of inner activities in relation to religious bahaviour. There are four types of tantra—*Kriya*, *Charya*, *Yoga* and *Anuttara yoga*.[2] Most of the Vajracharyas are not interested in other forms of tantra, and only practice *Kriya* tantra.

In ancient and medieval times, Patan became the center of tantric Buddhism and has remained so since ancient times. Ancient inscriptions have been found which mentioned *Viharas* such as Gum *Vihara*, Raj *Vihara*, Kharjurika *Vihara* and so on. But these references do not state where they were located. However, many prominent *Viharas* were in Patan. No archaeological excavations have been done, though. Ancient monolithic chaityas are still numerous in the Kathmandu Valley, but they do not provide enough information about the Lichhivi *Vihara*.

Almost all of the Vajrayana *Viharas* have three major, which include—

1. A principal deity called *Kwapadyo*.
2. A Chaitya.
3. A tantric shrine called *Agam*, on the first floor of the *Vihara*.

Native Buddhist scholars from Patan believed that features of both *Theravada* and *Mahayana* are integrated into the Vajrayana *Vihara*. According to this view, the principal deity itself is seen as part of the *Theravada* tradition but other pantheons are considered to be part of *Mahayana* Buddhism. In almost all of the Vajrayana *Viharas*, images of Sariputra and Mahamaudgalyayan are installed outside the main shrine.

Ratnakar Mahavihara is considered to be one of the most important *Viharas* in Patan, and is one of the fifteen main *Viharas* there. It is situated in the center of Patan. This *Vihara* originally stood at the Patan palace complex,[3] but was later moved to its present site. The king later established images of Siddhiganesh and Narsimha at the palace where this *Vihara* was originally located.[4] To commemorate this fact, a stone image of Buddha is displayed in a square water pot during the month of *Gumla*, when the image of Buddha is immersed. This practice is believed to represent the location of a Buddhist *Vihara* at that place. The *Vihara* is of course, *Hakha baha*. After this *Vihara* was moved to the present site, the Vajracharya lineage of *Hakha baha* left the *Sangha* and joined Bu *baha Sangha*. The two remaining Shakya lineages were given *Achaluyegu* initiation by the order of King Siddhi Narsimha Malla, so, the Vajracharya of the other *Sangha* accuse them of *Balan Acharya* (the Vajracharya which was conferred by order of the king). The Vajracharyas of *Hakha baha* do not accept this accusation. Sometimes, they use the term *Balan Acharya* to mean the good

Acharya (*Baalaan Acharya*),[5] but the *baha Sangha* members say that only those *Sangha* members who were adopted in the *Sangha* (*Thyaka masta*) received the *Achaluyegu* initiation under pressure from the Prime Minister. However, there is no documented evidence to prove this, even though it is a historical fact that two Shakya lineages were initiated and upgraded to the Vajracharya status by the order of the king. Another fact is that these Vajracharyas have no *Yajman* (patrons). Nor do they perform the *Karmakanda* (life-cycle) ritual. The *Sangha* members who left *Hakha baha* and joined the *Bu baha Sangha* are called *Rajpurohit Kawa* (royal priest lineage) in *Bu baha*. During *Agam puja* of *Sana Guthi* at *Hakha baha*, their role is still very important. The initiation of Shakya into Vajracharya status by the royal decree of a Malla king should be considered to be a distinct feature of this *baha Sangha*.

The Shakya community was divided into different categories during medieval times. They are Shakya *Bhikshu*, Sakha Shakya *Bhikshu*, *Brahmacharya Bhikshu* and *Chailaka Bhikshu*, but the present Buddhist *Sangha* members ignore these divisions. The tradition of the four day *Barechhoyegu* has become very popular. This ritual is very important in the Buddhist society, because it is the ritual which admits a boy into the *Sangha*. It also grants a boy with his caste status.[6] In *Hakha baha* most of the male children are given *Barechhoyegu* initiation between the ages of five and seven.

The *Achaluyegu* is another important rite that is performed at *Hakha baha*, which is the process through which one becomes a Vajracharya. After the initiation, one can conduct *Karmakanda* rites, so, this initiation is very important in Buddhist society. Not all the *Hakha baha Sangha* members receive the *Achaluyegu* initiation. The young generation is less interested in it, but it is optional.

Guthi is also a very important aspect of the activities in a *Vihara*. Several *Guthis* have operated so far in *Hakha baha Sangha*. The main *Guthis* are *Sangha bhojan Guthi, Sandey puja Guthi, Lainkya Bhu Guthi, Acha Guthi, Bicha Guthi, Sana Guthi* etc. The *Sangha* members do not need to join all the *baha Guthis*. There are only sixty-five members in the *Acha Guthi* as compared to one hundred fortyfive *Sangha* members. There are only twenty-five members in the *Bicha Guthi*. Many *Guthis* are similar to other *baha Guthis*, but the *Sandey puja Guthi* is a distinct type of *Guthi* in this *baha*. All male children born into the *Sangha* family, who have already undergone their rice-feeding ceremony within the year are given a ritual feast under this *Guthi*. There is no such *Guthi* in other *Bahas* in Patan.

Several *Puja* rituals are also performed in this *baha* on different occasions. Those *Pujas* include *Dau puja, Basundhara puja, Busadhan puja, Disi puja, Ja puja, Paphay puja, Chauchhayegu puja, Agam puja, Lokpala puja, Panchadana* etc. The *Sangha* members practice different types of religious activities, such as *Namasangiti, Pancharakshya* and Prajnaparamita recitations, and so on. In modern times, religion and religious practices have undergone several changes, so, the young generation is less interested in these things. Even the unstable income of the priesthood has certain connections with the waning of religious bahaviour.

This *baha* has a spiritual relationship with *Bu baha* and *Sri Baccha Vihara*, which are linked through certain ritual exchanges. In fact, *Hakha baha* has a long history with several unique characteristics, which made this *baha* different from other *bahas* in Patan. The tradition of *Kumari* in *Hakha baha* is also unique. Most of the Buddhist laity performs *Kumari puja* on several occasions. *Kumari* is worshipped during *Baha puja, Basundhara puja and Bungadyo Jatra*. If *Sangha* members organize a ceremony, they invite *Ajus* and *Kumari* to participate. They first offer *Dana* and a feast to *Kumari*, then to the *Ajus*. *Kumari* is a goddess who holds a higher position than that of the *Chakershwore*.

Hakha baha has a tradition of selecting eleven *Ajus*, instead of ten in other *Viharas*. They are known as *Chakreshwore* (*Thapanayaka*) *Nwokunayaka, Dakanayaka* and eight other *Nayakas*. Each stage of the *Bodhisattva bhumi* and *Paramita* are assigned to each *Aju* according to the position they hold in the hierarchy.

This *Vihara* consist of a group of five *Kacha baha*. The *Sangha* members are bound by rules and regulations and are also authorized to perform the *Barechhoyegu* initiation. All *Kacha baha* are built on the traditional model consisting of a chaitya and a small shrine.

There are different types of art work in this *baha*, which includes stone, wood, repousse and bronze. The main gate's concave tympanum is more spectacular than the stone art of other *Viharas*, and is very old. It can be assumed that this tympanum dates back to the old Vihara. The stone art found in other *Viharas* is from later periods. In this *Vihara*, the earliest stone *Shikharakut* Chaitya is very beautiful, and is dated N.S. 846. There are four *Dharmadhatu Mandalas*, two of which were mounted using repousse copper art. The big *Dharmadhatu Mandala* is also different from the *Mandalas* of other *Viharas* of Patan. There is a pair of stone statues of the donors, whose clothes and ornaments are from the medieval era. The other spectacular work of stone art is the statue of Manjusri, which is different from description of *Sadhanamala*. Manjushri is holding various attributes in her right and left hands, as mentioned in the text, but the head and colour are different from the textual description, as Manjushri is black. Similarly, Vajrasattwa and Basundhara are also painted black. These statues seem black just like Mauryan art pieces.

This *Vihara* has a Lichhivi Style white-washed chaitya. It is said that it was established before the *Vihara* was constructed. However, there is no evidence to prove this hypothesis. This chaitya is flanked by an image of serpents which rise from the quadrangles of the four pillars. This looks just as it does in the Guheshwori temple. It is a monolithic style chaitya, which is distinct from other chaityas.

Similarly, metal statues of Sariputra and Mahamaudgalyayana are kept on either side of the entrance of the main shrine. These statues are distinct components of this *baha*. Their clothes are translucent and their heads are disproportionate, so we can say that these images were influenced by the Gandhara School of Art. The *Prabhamandala*, however, is different from that of the Gandhara School.

Regarding the woodwork there are eight wooden tympanums, which depict different images of Vajrayana pantheons. All the tympanums are made of three wooden slabs. One of the tympanums depicts the Padmapani *Lokeshwore* in multicolour painting. The other tympanums are black. The wooden image of Padmapani *Lokeshwore* is kept on the left side of the *Kwapadyo*, and is said to be the oldest image in this *Vihara*. The *Ajus* said that the image is older than that of *Rato Machindranatha* (*Bungadyo*). But no date has been verified so far.

These *Viharas* were famous institutions in ancient times. The fact that the Tibetan *Guru* Marpa came to Nepal and took *Dekha* from Nepalese *Gurus* Paindapa and Chithrepa also helps to trace the history of this *Vihara*.[7] Upon his return after completing his education from *Siddha* Naropa, Marpa arranged an excellent *Ganachakra* (a ritual feast)[8] to express thanks to *Guru* Paindapa. Both *Guru* and disciple sang during that occasion to explain the meaning *Mahamudra*. The *Ganachakra* have been held at Ratnakar Mahavihara,[9] where Marpa lived for three years and studied tantra from the Nepalese *Gurus*. This highlights the popularity and scholastic tradition of Ratnakar Mahavihara as well as the tantric practices that were done there in the past.

Generally, *Hakha baha* is not different from other *Viharas* in Patan. The ignorance of *Vihara* committee members about the importance of historical documents and other records (*dhalapau*) has had a direct effect on the writing of history. Their orthodox attitude and reluctance to open such old books really hampered efforts to write an authentic and detailed history of this *baha*. This ultimately leads a complete loss of historical knowledge and history of Vajrayana in Nepal.

References

1. Gokarna inscription of Amshuvarma mentions the term *Vajrayana*. Dhanavajra Vajracharya, *Lichhavikalin Abhilekh*, Kirtipur: INAS, 2030 B.S., pp. 370- 71.
2. Wangchuk Dorjee Negi: *Vajrayana Darshana Evam Sadhana*, Varanasi: Central Institute of Higher Tibetan Studies, 1998, pp. 121-32.
3. Daniel Wright: *History Of Nepal* Translated from Parbatiya, Calcutta: Low Price Publication, 1877, p. 159.

4. John K. Locke: *Buddhist Monasteries of Nepal*, Kathmandu: Sahayogi Press, 1985, pp. 21-27.
5. Informed by Late *Aju* Pushpa Raj Vajracharya of *Hakha baha*.
6. John K. Locke: 'Newar Buddhist Initiation Rites', *Contribution to Nepalese Studies*, Vol. II, No. 2, 1975, p. 14.
7. Shakya, f. n. no 1, pp. 31-32.
8. *Kriyasamucchaya* defines the term as a sacramental circle, which is without a female partner. It is the meeting of rice secum, but for Newars, it is a ritual or sacramental meal after rituals. *Also see:* S.C Das, *Indian Pandits in the Land of Snow*, Calcutta: K.L. Mukhopadhyaya, 1965, p. 77.
9. Shakya, f. n. no. 1, p. 32.

GLOSSARY

Achaluyegu:	The Initiation rite of the Vajracharyas, consisting of the five consecrations.
Acharya Guthi:	The Guthi association of the Vajracharyas.
Agam:	A secret ritual room where the secret tantric deities are placed.of the Newars is performed.
Ajus:	The elders of the *baha*.
Aarti Puja:	Offering of light in the evening.
Ashta matrika:	The eight mother goddesses worshipped by both Hindus and Buddhists. Their eight shrines surrounding the towns and cities of the valley and thus delimit the sacred space of the town.
Avadana:	The glorious acts of the Buddha or Bodhisattvas described in the form of stories.
Baha:	Newari terminology for Buddhist monastery.
Bahi:	A type of *Vihara* which is different from *baha*, whose members are known as *Brahmacharya Bhikshu.*
Bahidya Boyegu:	Exhibition of deities in *Bahi's Viharas.*

Bare:	The term used for the members of *baha Sangha.*
Barechhoyegu:	The initiation rite after which one enters the *Sangha* as a new member.
Betaju:	An official secretary of *Sangha* who prepares the list of *Dyopala* and maintains the record of various feasts.
Bhikshu:	Buddhist monk. In Newari Buddhism a *Sangha* member claims himself as the monk. Newar Buddhism has no tradition of monkhood.
Buddha:	The enlightened one, the Buddha.
Busadhan:	Birth day.
Chaitya:	A stupa which represents the mind aspect of Buddha.
Chakresvara:	Seniormost member of the *baha Sangha*.
Chamo:	A fan made of yak tail.
Dekha:	Spiritual initiation in which mantra is given by the officiating Vajracharya priest..
Dekhachayakyagu:	Opening of God's *puja* ceremony.
Dhyamamanjari:	A symbol of abundance of wealth.
Dharma:	Buddha's teachings.
Dharmadhatu Mandala:	Mandala of Manjushri which is enshrined in all the *bahas*.
Digi:	Prayer room in Vihara used as the meeting place by the elders.
Digu puja:	Annual worship of the lineage deity.
Dyopala:	The attending priest at the baha main shrine.
Ghanta:	Bell.
Gumla Dharma:	A religious observances observed during the sacred month of *Gumla* (July-August).
Guthi:	Newar social organization that ensures

	continued observance of social and religious customs; or institutional land grant.
Guthiyar:	A member of Guthi.
Homa:	The ritual sacred fire.
Jajman:	Patron.
Kachabaha:	Branch Vihara.
Kwapadyo:	Main deity in the *baha*.
Mahavihara:	The great monastery.
Nini:	Father's sister.
Nitya *puja*:	Daily worship.
Panchadana:	Offering donation of five kinds of materials. - Phenomenon
Puja:	The act of worship.
Sana Guthi:	A Guthi managing funeral rite of Sangha members.
Sangha:	Members of Vihara.
Shakha baha:	The branch monastery.
Sthavir:	An elder.
Thapa Aju:	The head of the *Sangha*.
Tympanum:	A semi-circle decorative panel over the doorway of a temple.
Upasaka:	A lay believer.
Vajra:	Thunderbolt which is a ritual object symbolizing voidness.
Vajracharya:	Newar Buddhists priest. Literally, the Master of the Vajra.
Vajradhatu Mandala:	A misnomer for a *Dharmadhatu Mandala* surmounted by a Vajra.
Vamsavali:	Chronicle.
Varad Mudra:	A gesture of giving.
Yagyashala:	A sacred pit used to perform the rituals of fire sacrifice.

रत्नाकर महाविहारको शीलालेखहरु

APPENDIX No. 1

ॐ नमो शाकय मुनय नमः सम्वत ७९३ कार्तिक शुक्ल पूर्णमासय् थ्व दिनस जजमान ग्वनिराज भारोमया भार्या भुवनीजु थ्वनिम्ह समेत ङमसेन.....स्तनं दुन्ता श्री शाक्यमुनि सके सास्त्र सनेगु...जुरो ॥ थन भाषानं शुकि माज दुन्ताजुरो निहदत्त...

(अक्षर पढ्न नसकिने)

APPENDIX No. 2

ऊँ नमो बुद्धायः॥ नेपारे, सम्मते वर्षे ॥ गनन, बिन्दु, बसु गदिने ॥ अस्मिन बर्षे माघशिते अग्नि तिथि नारायन नक्षत्रे ॥ राषियोगे सोमबारसरे यवदिने प्रतिस्था कृते एवं रश्मिवन महाविहारा निवासित चक्रेश्वरि भी चन्द्रमुनि जु, श्री वासिंजु श्री जिव चन्द्रजु, भी देवसिहजु, श्री बज्रपानिजु, श्री कनकजु, श्री देवजु, श्री सम्बर देवजु, श्री घरजु, श्री सिक्षमुनिजु, श्री घरजु पनि दश पारमिता प्रमुखस सं मुहन श्री रथंजु, श्री बज्रपानिजु बराया, मुरमि (मुल्मि) काशिरामजु समुह याङाओ थ्वते स्वम्ह प्रमुखनं चिन्तायाङाओ थ्वहतखू वाहारसं रुपक्षे.या रसं थुनिथायसं अतवन सियाव जुर गोविन्द राय भारो श्रयोस्तु सम्वत ८०१ सके धंक पादुकुन्हु प्रतिस्था याङाजुई ॥

APPENDIX No. 3

ऊँ नमो भगवत्यै ः॥ विश्वभद्र जिनबुद्ध विश्व भद्र जगत गुरु विश्वनाथ सदावन्दे विश्वमूर्ति निरुपतां ॥०॥ स्वस्ति नेपाराव्दे बसु, ऋृतु, नागे ज्येष्ठ कृष्पा दुतिया पर तृतियान्तिथौ .... ढायन उत्तराषाढा नक्षेत्रे ब्रम्हयोगे गुरुवासरे तीन्दने श्री लक्ष्मी वन्त महाविहार भूमि इष्टिकाभि : सुनिर्मिता दानपति पीरदेव चिकितिना भार्या रषधनी : स्तथा चिपातक कुदुन नास्ति॥०॥ स्वस्ति सम्वत् ८६८ शुद्ध कृष्ण द्वितियापर तृतिया के प्रतिष्ठा याङा दानपति शाक्यवंश पति देना चिकिधीनेम्ह फुर्कीजनचेक अ बँसिया जुलो ॥०॥ थ्व बिहारस बजिल्हुइमदु माथ वंगुथासय् वंक्वयाद मदु ॥ च्वलय फइचिइ मदु थरपा वम्हङा संछि समोहन धाय् याथमदु, (यस्को तल पढ्न नसकिने) ......पञ्च महापाप लाईकथहं या जुल ।

APPENDIX No. 4

ऊँ नमो श्री शाक्यमुनय ॥ ऊँ नमो बुद्धाय ॥ ऊँ नमो धर्माय ॥ ऊँ नमो संघाय नमो नमः ॥ श्रयोस्तु सम्वत ९५९ चैत्रमासे शुक्लपक्षे पूर्णस्थातिथौ उत्तर फाल्गुणि नक्षत्रे बृद्धि योगे शुक्रवासरे मीनराशि सवित्रतरि सिंहराशिगते चन्द्रमासि श्री ३ लक्ष्मि कल्याण वर्मण संस्कारित लक्ष्मि वर्ण महाविहार श्री ३ शाक्यमुनि बुद्ध भगवान या देओर जिर्णोद्धार याङाओ प्रतिस्था याना दिन जुल। स्वस्ति श्री चक्र चुडामनि श्री ३ राजराजेन्द्र विक्रम शाहदेव महाराज या पर्यायस्, थ्ववेलस हःखवहाया श्री चक्रेश्वरी थरपा श्री धर्मसिंजु प्रमुख नाय्क श्री धर्म मुनिजु, श्री भाजु पतिजु, श्री चीधिजु, श्री शिरिजु, श्री भाजुधंसिहजु, श्री भाजु धंजु, श्री तःधि धंजु, श्री धनभाईजु, श्री विरनन्दजु, श्री भाजुभनिजु, थ्वतेनायक प्रभृति सकल संघ समूहन जिर्णेद्वारा याना जुरो ॥ भूया चिन्ता याकजन सर्वसधाया थकारि श्री जयमुनिजु श्री भिर धारजु, श्री मुनिन्द्रजु, श्री धनओन्त सिंहजु, श्री सतमुनिजु थ्वतेजना चिन्ता याङाओ, श्री ३ भगवान या देओर जिर्णोद्धार याना प्रतिस्था यानादिन जुरो।

ऊँ नमोः रत्न त्रयायः। ऊँ नमो बाज्रसत्वायः ॥ नमः बसुन्धरायः ॥ नमः मञ्जु नाथायः ॥।

APPENDIX No. 5

श्रयोस्तु ॥ शशि, बसु, निधि, सरख्यौर्मित सम्वत् ९८१ सरे माघमासे कृष्ण पक्षे तृतियान्तिथौ हस्तानक्षत्रे शुलपरगण्ड योगे बुधबासरे कुम्भराशिगते सवितरे कन्याराशिगते चन्द्रमशि ॥ एवस्मित शुभदिने ॥ ललितापुर महानगरान्तर्वर्ति श्री लक्ष्मी कल्याण वर्मण संस्कारित श्री लक्ष्मी वर्ण महाविहारस नैत्रनृत्य कोणे दिगस तोरण सहितद्वार स्वंगुलि श्री बज्रसत्व, श्री बसुन्धरा, श्री मञ्जुश्री थ्वते स्वम्ह देवताया मूर्तिदयका दुदु वन्ला गृह निवाशित बज्राचार्य योगनरसिंह जुया...... सकल परिवारया धर्मचित्त उत्पति जुयाव धर्म, अर्थ, काम, मोक्ष, जगत संसार उद्धार कामना यास्य थ्वेत स्वम्ह देवता पूजा, बुसाधं, आचार्य गुठिमा निमित्त सहित आयस्ताया निति १ रोवजब २ इकुहिति बुं ॥ भूय कर्ष १ भनिको बुं दामतका ५१ अघलि प्रीतियाङाओ आचार्य गुठिस दुन्ता जुल । ॐ नमो रत्न त्रयाय .... ।

APPENDIX No. 6

श्रयोस्तु सम्वत १००० पौषमासस एतत् दिने श्री ५ महाराजाधिराज सुरेन्द्रविक्रम शाहदेव महाराजा प्रज्यायस श्री ३ लक्ष्मीकल्याण वर्मण संस्कारित रत्नाकर महाविहार स-विराजित श्री ३ शाक्यमुनि भगवान या देओल या पौलःस्याङा ओ सयवलक्ष्मी वर्ण महाविहारया चक्रेश्वरी धलपा, नाय्कजु प्रभृति संघसमोहन चिन्ता याङाओ जिर्णउद्धार याङादिन जुरो ॥ पुनः भाषा सम्वत् १०१३ कृष्णमासे शुक्लपक्षे ज्येष्ठभ्यांतिथौः मेघा नक्षत्रेः व्याघात् योगे मंगलवारसरे वृषराशिगते श्री सूर्यसिंह राशिगते चन्दैमशि एतत् दिने श्री ५ महाराजाधिराज श्री पृथ्वीवीर विक्रम शाहदेव महाराजा या प्रज्यायस सयव श्री ३ लक्ष्मी कल्याण वर्मण संस्कारित रत्नाकर महाविहारया शाक्यमुनि भगवान दथुधोल त्वार लुंक्षननिया छें वङाओ प्रतिस्था याङा दिनजुलोः थ्ववेलस एवं लक्ष्मीवर्ण महाविहारया चक्रेश्वरी थपाजु श्री दिन सिंहजु प्रमुखं नाय्कजु, श्री घओसिंहजु, कुरओन्तसिंहजु, श्रीहर्षजु, श्री तेजवीरजु, श्री धिवसिंह जु, श्री चीधं जु, श्री हर्ष जु, श्री व्यषा सिंहजु, श्रमान् जु, श्री जोति राज जु, थ्वते नाय्क जु प्रभृति, संघसमोहन चिन्ता याङाओ, छें दनाओ प्रतिस्था याना दिन जुरो । एतत् पुण्यानु भावेन लोकासन्तु सुखावर्त्या शुथ ।

APPENDIX No. 7

नमो शाक्यसिंहायः ॥ सम्वत १०२५ भ्फि ज्येष्ठमास कृष्ण पक्षे पूर्वाषाढा नक्षत्रे शुभयोगे बुधवासरे धनुराशिगत सवितरे मकरराशिगत चन्द्रमशि एतत् दिने श्री ५ महाराजा श्री पृथ्वी वीर विक्रम महाराजया पर्यायस श्री ३ लक्ष्मी वर्ण महाविहार पूर्वपती च्वनेगु छें च्वनीपिं न्हना वनाओ श्री भगवान या दांमनं थ्व छें दयकाओ प्रतिस्था यानाजुल। थन भाषा १०२७ भ्फि चैत्र शुदि३सल्वहँधोकयाङओचानंजिर्णउद्धार याङाजुलु। पिने राक्षिसं चिकं अतनं बँ सिया जुल। थ्ववे लस जुयाओ च्वंपिं लक्ष्मी वर्ण महाविहार या चक्रेश्वरी श्री धनओन्त सिंहजु, थः पा श्री तेजवीर, दाका श्री लखवीरजु, पञ्चस्थवीर श्री हर्षजोति जु, श्री हर्षमान जु, नायक श्रीभिमराज जु, श्रीगजवीर जु, श्री भाजुवीर जु, श्री बज्रराज जु, श्री थपराज जु, श्री हर्ष धंजु, थुतिनायक जु या सर्वसंघ समोहन जुयाओ सम्वत १०२८ भ्फि भाद्र शुक्ल १५रोज पस समस्त दयकाओ प्रतिष्ठा याना जुल थुगु धर्म नं जगत संसार उद्धार जुय माल शुभमस्तु मंगल सर्वदा, शुभम् ॥

APPENDIX No. 8

श्रयोस्तु सम्वत १०३५ भ्रि अधिक वैशाख शुक्ल षष्ठमि आद्रानक्षत्र अतिगन्ध योग मंगलवारसरे मेषराशिगत वृषराशिगत सवितर मिथुन राशिगत चन्द्र थ्वखुहुसं लक्ष्मीवर्ण महाविहार तुंननिसं लं समेत फातनं लाय्बँनं सिया जुल। थुकेयादानपति सयव वाहालय बज्राचार्य हर्षजोति, प्रमुख नं सजिव सकुलोत्पन्न भ्रातृ द्वितीय हर्षधंजु, भ्रातृ तृतिया दयांमुनि, चतुर्थ भ्रातृ पञ्चमुनि, पञ्चम भ्रातृया काय् शिर पति प्रथम भार्या हेरामाया, द्वितिय भार्या चिलानि चतुर्थ शुनषा धर्मलानि, पञ्चम शुनषा पुनमाया, थ्वतेजहान सकल समोहन धर्मचित्त उत्पत्ति जुयाव तुंननि स लाय्बँ सियाजुल हर्षजोतिया जहान सकसिनं दोहलपा जुल थुगु धर्म नं. जगत संसार उद्धार जुय माल .... संप्तवृद्धि परि............पूर्ण जुयाओ थुगुलि कृति सर्वदा काल स्थिर जुय माल।

APPENDIX No. 9

ॐ नमो श्री बज्रसत्वायः ॥

श्रयोस्तु सम्वत १०५४ पौष मासे कृष्णपक्षे अमावस्यां तिथौ थ्व खुल्हुया दिनस भूमिकम्प जुयाओ लक्ष्मीवर्ण रत्नाकर महाविहार स श्रीशाक्यमुनि भगवानया देवालय दुनाओ सम्वत १०५५ माघस शुक्लपक्षया अष्टम्यां तिथौ थ्वखुल्हुया दिंनसं निस्यं जिर्णउद्धार याना हया दिन जुल, श्री त्रिभुवन वीर विक्रम शाहदेव या पर्यायस दयका जुर, थ्वविहार या चक्रेश्वर थकालि श्रीबुद्धिमान जु, श्रीव्यषासिंजु, श्री हर्षराजजु, श्रीसिद्धिराजजु, श्रीरत्नजोतिजु, श्रीदेवजोतिजु, श्रीमान्जोतिजु, श्रीहर्षमानजु, श्रीहर्षराजजु, श्रीपञ्चमुनिजु, श्रीत्रैलोक्य मुनजि, वेताजु श्रीधर्मराजजु, थ्वते नायक जु आदिसर्वसंघ समोहन देवालय जिर्णोद्धार सम्पूर्ण सिधयकाओ सम्वत १०५६ ज्येष्ठ मासे शुक्ल पक्षे पञ्चम्यां तिथौ पुनर्वसु पर तिष्य नक्षत्र सोमबार सरे दिनस शास्त्रोक्त विधिथ्य देवाधि प्रतिस्था शान्तिकर्म मात्र याना जुल, थुगु जिर्णउद्धार स ग्वहालि याकपिं दाता आदि चक्रेश्वर सर्वसंघ पिनि इहलोक सुखसम्पतिलाना परलोके मोक्षगतिलाय माल जुलः ॥ हाकनं थुगु धर्म चतुर्योनि जन्मजुया च्वंको सकल जगत संसार उद्धार जुयमाल शुभम् ॥

* * *

SELECT BIBLIOGRAPHY

Documentary Sources

- Inscriptions of *Hakha Baha* (Ratnakar Mahavihara of Patan).

Unpublished Dissertations

- Pradhan, Sushila: *Buddhism in Ancient Nepal* (Ph.D. Dissertation submitted to the Faculty of Humanities and Social Science) Tribhuvan University, Kathmandu: 1998.
- Vajracharya, Indra Kumari: *Cultural Heritage of Lakshmi Kalyana Varma Sanskarita Ratnakara Mahavihara of Patan* (Unpublished thesis submitted to PGD Buddhist Studies Programme) Tribhuvan University, 2001.
- Vajracharya, Ranjana: *Role of the Hiranyavarna Mahavihara in Socio-cultural life of the Buddhist Newars* (Ph.D. Dissertation Submitted to the Faculty of Humanities and Social Sciences) Tribhuvan University, Kathmandu: 2050 B.S.

Books in English

- Allen, Michael R.: *The Cult of Kumari Virgin Worship in Nepal*, Kathmandu: Institute of Nepal and Asian Studies 1975.
- Bamerjee, Anukul Chandra: *Aspects Of Buddhist Culture From Tibetan Source*, Calcutta: Firma K.L. Mukhopadhyaya (p.) Ltd., 1984.
- Bapat, P. V.: *2500 Years of Buddhism*, New Delhi: Ministry of Information and Broadcasting, 1997.
- Basak, Radha Govinda: *Lectures on Buddha and Buddhism*, Calcutta, Sambodhi Publications, 1961.

- Bhattacharya, Benoytosh: *The Indian Buddhist Iconography*, Calcutta: K.L.Mukhopadhyaya, 1968.
- *Bhikshu* Susobhan: *Buddhism At A Glance*, Kathmandu, Anandakuti Trust, 1985.
- Brown, Percy : *Picturesque Nepal*, London: Adam and Charles Black, 1912.
- Butler, Edward C., *Benedictive Monachism*, Oxford, Oxford University Press, 1966.
- Chen, Keneth K.S.: *Buddhism: The Light of Asia*, New York, Barren's Educational Series, 1968.
- Chetty, Derawas: *The Desert A City*, Oxford, Oxford University Press, 1966.
- Conze, Edward: *Buddhism: Its Essence and Development*, New York, Harper & Row, 1975.
- Crystal Mirror Book, *Light of liberation : A History of Buddhism in India*, Vol. VII, Berkley: Dharma Publishing 1992.
- Davis, T.W Rhys and H. Oldenberg (tr.): *Vinaya* text III, Maxmuller (ed.), *The Sacred Book of the East*, Vol. XX, New Delhi: Motilal Benarasi Das, 1975
- Dutt, Nalinaksha: *Early Monastic Buddhism,* Calcutta, J.C. Sarkhel, 1941.
- Dutt, Nalinaksha: *Early Monastic Buddhism*, Calcutta, K. L. Mukhopadhyaya, 1971.
- Dutt, Sukumar: *Early Buddhist Monachism*, London, Kegan Paul, 1924.
- Dutt, Sukumar: *Buddhist Monks and Monasteries in India*, London, Allen & Unwin, 1962.
- Dutta, N. and K. D. Bajpai: *Development of Buddhism in Uttar Pradesh*, Lucknow: Publication Bureau of Government of Uttar Pradesh, 1956.
- *Echoes From Mt. Kaya*, seoul, Lotus Lantern International Buddhist Center, 1988.
- Eliade, Mercia, (ed.): *The Encyclopaedia of Religion*, Vol. 10, New York, MacMillan Co.
- Geiger, Wilhelm (Eng.tr.): *The Mahavamsha or the Great Chronicle of Ceylon*, New Delhi: Asian Educational Services, 1986.
- Gellner, David : *Monk, Householder And Tantric Priest*, Delhi: Foundation Books, 1996.
- Ghuraye, G.S. : *The Indian Sadhus*, Bombay, Asia Publishing House, 1964.

- Gombrich, Richard : 'Introduction to the Buddhist Way, in Heinz Bechert (ed.), *The World of Buddhism*, London, Thames and Hudson, 1984.
- Kern, H. : 'Saddharmapundarika Sutra' in Friedrich Maxmuller (ed.), *The Sacred Books of The East*, Vol. 21. New Delhi, Motilal Benarasi Dass, 1925.
- Hackamann, H.: *Buddhism as a Religion*, Delhi, Neeraj Publications, 1981.
- Hastings, James (ed.): *The Encyclopaedia of Religion and Ethics*, New York, T. and T. Clark, 1981.
- Humphrey, Christmas: *Buddhism: An Introduction & Guide*, London: Penguin Books, 1962.
- Jha, M., *Aspects of Traditional City of Janakpur*. Patna, Kitabmahal, 1979.
- Joshi, Shankar Lal: *Amshuvarma*, New Delhi. Anmol Publications, 1993.
- Kitagawa, Joseph M.: *Religions of the East*, Philadelphia, West Minster, n.d.
- Knowles, David: *The Monastic Order In England*, Cambridge, Cambridge University Press, 1963.
- Kolver, Bernard and Hemraj Shakya: *Documents From Rudravarna—Mahavihara Patan: Sales and Mortgage*, Sanskrit: VGH Wissenschaftsverlag, 1985.
- Lama, Dalai: *Short Essays on Buddhist Thought & Practice*, Dharmashala, Secretariat of H.H. Dalai Lama, 1982.
- Lee Jong Ik: 'Problems of Vinaya to Monks and Nuns in the Modern world', in Lee Sun Keun and Rhi Ki Young (ed.), *Buddhism and Modern World*, Seoul, Dongguk University Press, 1976.
- Lock, John K.: *Buddhist Monasteries of Nepal*, Kathmandu: Sahayogi Press, 1985.
- Lock, John K.: *Karunamaya* (The Cult of Avalokiteswar Matsyendranath in the Valley of Nepal), Kathmandu: Sahayogi Prakashan, 1980.
- Locke, John K.: *Unique Features of Buddhism*, in Tadeus Skoropski (ed.), *The Buddhist Heritage*, Tring, Institute of Buddhist Studies, 1989.
- Marriot, McKim: 'Little Communities in an Indigenous Civilization', Marriot (ed.), *Village India*, Chicago, The Chicago University Press, 1958.

- Mishra, G.S.P.: *The Age of Vinaya*, New Delhi, Munshi Ram Manohar Lal, 1972.
- Narada, Thera : *The Buddha and His Teachings*, Malaysia: Buddhist Missionary Society, 1988.
- Negi, Wangchuk Dorjee: *Vajrayana Darshan Evam Sadhana*, India: Central Institute of Higher Tibetan Studies, 1998.
- Oldenberg, H.: *The Buddha*, W. Hoey (tr.), London, 1904.
- Pachow, W.: *A Comparative Study of Pattimokha*, Shantiniketan, the Sino-Indian Cultural Society, 1955.
- Petech, Luciano: *Medieval History of Nepal*, Rome, IsMEO, 1984.
- Rajendra Ram: *History of Buddhism in Nepal 704-1396,* Patna: Gyan Bharati Prakashan, 1977.
- Regmi, D. R.: *Medieval Nepal*, Calcutta: K. L. Mukhopadhyaya, 1966.
- Regmi, D. R.: *Ancient Nepal*, Calcutta: K. L. Mukhopadhyaya, 1960.
- Regmi, Dilli Raman: *Ancient & Medieval Nepal*, Kathmandu: n.p, 1952.
- Regmi, Dilli Raman: *Medieval Nepal*, Calcutta: K.L. Mukhopadhya, 1965.
- Rijal, Babu Krishna: *Archaeological Remains of Kapilvastu, Lumbini and Devdaha*, Kathmandu: Educational Enterprises, 1979.
- Roerich, George N.: *The Blue Annals*, New Delhi: Motilal Benarsi Dass, 1996.
- Roerich, George N.: *Biography of Dharmaswamin* (Chag- Lo-tsa-ba Chos-rje- dPal), Patna: K.P. Jayasawal Institute, 1959.
- Sankhalia, Hansmukh D.: The University of Nalanda, Madras, B. G. Paul, 1934.
- Sankrityayan, Rahul: *Vinayapitaka*, Varanasi, Mahabodhi Society, 1935.
- Shakya, Min Bahadur, *A Short History of Buddhism in Nepal*, Lalitpur: Young Buddhist Publication, 1986.
- Shakya, Min Bahadur: *Princess Bhrikuti Devi*, Delhi: Book Faiths India, 1977.
- Shakya, Min Bahadur: *The Iconography of Nepalese Buddhism*, Kathmandu: Handicraft Association of Nepal, 1999.
- Shastri, N. Aiwaswamy : 'Approach To Hinduism', in P.V. Bapat (ed.), *2500 Years of Buddhism*, New Delhi, Ministry of Information and Broadcasting, 1959.
- Sircar, D.C.: *Inscriptions of Ashoka,* New Delhi: Ministry of Information and Broadcasting, 1998.

- Snellgrove, David L.: *Tibetan Buddhism* , Vol. II, Boston: Sambhala Publications, 1987.
- Spiro, Melford E.: *Buddhism and Society: A Great Tradition and Its Burmese Vicissitudes*, Berkeley, The University of California Press, 1982.
- Stevension, Margaret Sinclair: *The Heart Of Jainism*, London, Oxford University Press, 1915.
- Suzuki, Daisez Teitaro, *An Introduction to Zen*, New York, Grover Press, 1964.
- Tambiah, S.J.: *Buddhism and the Spirit Cult in North-East Thailand*, Cambridge, Cambridge University Press, 1970.
- Thapa Shanker: *'Monasticism in Korean Buddhism'*, Seoul, 1989, unpublished preliminary research report submitted to the International Cultural Society of Korea.
- Thapa, Shanker: *Buddhist Monasticism in Theory and Practice*, Kathmandu: Walden Book House, 1995.
- The Cullavagga Vol. VI, No. 2, T.W. Rhys Davis and H. Oldenberg (tr.), Vinaya Texts III, Maxmuller (ed.)., *The Sacred Books of the East*, Vol. XX, New Delhi, Motilal Benarasi Dass, 1975.
- *The Encyclopaedia Britannica*, Vol. 12, Chicago, Helen Hemingway, Benton, 1978.
- *The New Encyclopaedia Britannica,* Vol. II, Chicago, Helen Hemingway Bentom, 1979.
- *The Seeker's Glossary of Buddhism*, New York: Sutra Translation Committee of U.S.A and Canada 1998.
- Thera, N. and K. Thera : *The Mirror Of Dhamma*, Colombo, A.B. Ggomes Trust, 1975.
- Thomas, E. J.: *The History of Buddhist Thought*, New York, Barnes and Noble, 1951.
- Thomas, Walters: *On Yuanchwang's Travel in India,* Vol. 1, New Delhi: Munshiram Manoharlal Publisher, 1973.
- Vaidya, Karunakar: *Buddhist Tradition And Culture Of Kathmandu*, Lalitpur: Sajha Prakashan, 1986.
- Vajracharya, Dhanavajra and Kamal Prakash Malla: *The Gopalrajvamsavali,* Kathmandu: Franz Steiner and Nepal Research Center, 1985.
- Vidyarthi, L. P., M. Jha and B. N. Saraswati, *The Sacred Complex of Kashi*, New Delhi, Popular, Publication, 1979.
- Warren, H. C.: *Buddhism in Translations,* New York, Atheneum, 1963.

- Wright, Daniel *History of Nepal,* Translated from Parbatia, Calcutta: Sushil Gupta, 1958.

Books in Nepali

- *Bhasavamsavali*, Vol. 1, Kathmandu: Deptt. of Archaeology, 1963.
- *Bhasavamsavali*, Vol. 2, Kathmandu, Nepal National Library, 2023 .
- Bhikshu Sudarshan, *Nepalya Bouddha Dharma*, Vol. 1, Kathmandu, 1982.
- Bhikshu Sudarsan: *Nepali Vihara Ka Bisrstaharu,* Lalitpura: Sradhaluharu, 2040.
- Gywali, Surya Vikram: *Nepal Upatyaka ko Madhyakalin Itihasa*, Kathmandu: Royal Academy 2019, B.S.
- Joshi, Hari Ram: *Himjwala*, Lalitpur: The author, 2026 V.S.
- Joshi, Hari Ram: *Nepalko Prachin Abhilekh,* Kathmandu: Royal Nepal Academy, 2030 B.S.
- Newami, Dalsha: *Samyak Mahadan Parva Sankshipta Parichaya* (A Brief Introduction To Samyak Mahadana Festival), Kathmandu: Dharma Ratna Shakya, 1993.
- Pradhan, Bhuvan Lal (tr.): *Buddhavamsha* (Newari), Kathmandu: Jnanaratna Kamsakar, 2057 B.S.
- Rajvamshi, Shankar Man: *Bhumi Sambandhi Tadpatra*, Part 1, Kathmandu: Rashtriya Abhilekhalaya, 2040 B.S.
- Regmi, Jagdish Chandra: *Nepal Ko Dharmik Itihas*, Kathmandu: Ratna Pustak Bhandar, 2039 B.S.
- Shakya, Mahendra: *Budhi Raj Vajracharya ko Sankshipta Jivani,* Lalitpur: Yashodhara Mahavihara Sudhar Samiti, 2058 B.S.
- Shakya, Mahendra: *Basundhara Devi Ek Adhyayan,* Lalitpur: Lotus Research Center, 2051 B.S.
- Tewari, Ramji: *et.al*, *Abhilekh Sangraha*, Kathmandu: Itihas Samsodhan Mandal, 2020 B.S.
- Vajracharya, Bhadra Ratna (ed.): *Dhanavajra Vajracharya ka Aitihasik Lekh Sangraha*, Vol. 1, Lalitpur, Hera Devi Shakya, 2056, B.S.
- Vajracharya, Dhanavajra and K. P. Malla: *The Gopalrajvamsavali*, Kathmandu: Nepal Research Center, 1985.
- Vajracharya, Dhanavajra: *Madhyakalin Abhilekh*, Kirtipur, Center for Nepal and Asian Studies, 2056, B.S.
- Vajracharya, Dhanavajra, *Licchivikal ka Abhilekh*, Kathmandu: Institute of Nepal and Asian Studies, 2030 B.S.

- Vajracharya, Dunda Bahadur: *Purna Bahadur Vajracharya: 'A Tribute To His Life & Work*, Patan: Bir Purna Pustak Sangrahalaya, 1996.
- Vajracharya, Herakazi : *Nepalko Boauddha Dharmama Basundhara Devi,* Lalitpur, Buddhi Raj and Mim Maya Bajracharya, 2058 B.S.
- Vajracharya, Herakazi: *Yashodhara Mahavihara Sangha,* Lalitpur: Buddha Jayanti Samaroha Samiti, 2050, B.S.
- Vajracharya, Prakash: *Bauddha Darpan*, Kathmandu: Dharmakriti Prakashan, 1996.

Books in Newari

- Vajracharya, Ranjana: *Panchadana Bauddha Parva*, Kathmandu: Shakya Ja, 2000.
- Shakya, Hem Raj: *Bauddha Murti Chhagu Adhyayan,* Kathmandu: Khwaspusa, 1091 N.S.
- Shakya, Hem Raj : *Maniggal Rajprasada,* Kathmandu: Buddha Jayanti Samaroh Samiti, 2518 Buddha Samvat.
- Shakya, Hem Raj : *Rudra Varna Mahavihara Chhagu Adhyayan*, Lalitpur: Buddha Jayanti Samaroh Samiti, 2051 B.S.
- Shakya, Hem Raj : *Samyak Mahadan Guthi*, Kathmandu: Jagat R. Tuladhar, 1100 N.S.
- Shakya, Hem Raj : *Swayambhu Mahachaitya*, Kathmandu: Swayambhu Bikas Mandala, 1098 N.S.
- Shakya, Min Bahadur (ed.): *Arya Gunakarandavyuha Sutra* (Newari), Lalitpur: Nagarjuna Institute Exact Methods, 1997.
- Shakya, Min Bahadur and Purna Harsha Vajracharya (ed.), *Swayambhu Purana*, Lalitpur, Nagarjuna Institute of Exact Methods, 2058 B.S.
- Vajracharaya, Ratna Kaji and Vijay Raj: *Newa Deya Tacha*, Kathmandu: The authors, 2039 B.S.
- Vajracharya, Badri Ratna : *Swayambhu Mahapuran*, Kathmandu: Sanu Maya Tuladhar, 1103 N.S.
- Vajracharya, Hirakaji, *Guthi Bahi Vihara Sangha ya Chhagu Adhyayan*, Lalitpur: Dipawali Pustkalaya, 1999.
- Vajracharya, Hirakaji : *Yalaya Bauddha Vihara*, Lalitpur: Bauddha Vihara Sangha, 2057 B.S.
- Vajracharya, Hirakaji : *Yashodhar Mahavihara Sangha Chhagu Adhyayan,* Lalitpur: Buddha Jayanti Samaroh Samiti, 2050 B.S.
- Vajracharya, Nisthananda (tr.), *Lalitvistara Sutra*, Lalitpur, Youngmen Buddhist Association, 1978.
- Vajracharya, Ratna Kaji: *Yandeya Bauddha Puja Kriya Ya Halajvala*, Kathmandu: Nepal Buddha Prakashan, N.S 1100.

- Vajracharya, Suryaman: *Ratnakar Mahavihara ya Sankshipta Parichaya*, Yala: Dhusa Jyasa, N.S 1116.
- Vajracharya, Badri Ratna: *Nhapayapim Prasiddha Vajracharyapim*, Swayambhu: Ananda Kuti Vihara Trust, 2046 B.S.

Books in Hindi

- Sankrityayan, Rahul: *Vinayapitaka*, Taiwan: the Corporate Body of the Buddha Education Foundation, n.d.
- Sashani, Thinley Ram Das: *Vajrayana Darhsana Evam Sadhna,* Sarnath: Central Institute of Higher Tibetan Studies, 1998.
- Upadhyaya, Basudeva: *Prachin Bhartiya Stupa,* Patna: Hindi Granth Academy, 1972.

Journal Articles in English

- Allen, Michael: 'Buddhism Without Monks: The Vajrayana Religion of the Newars of Kathmandu Valley', *South Asia,* No. 2, 1972.
- Bechert, Heinz and Hartman Jens-Uwe: 'Observation on the Reforms of Buddhism in Nepal', *Journal of Nepal Research Center*, Vol. VIII, 1988.
- Bernier, Ronald M. 'Notes on Chusya Bahal in Kathmandu', *Kailash* Vol. VI, No. 4, 1978.
- Decleer, Hubert: 'Sacred Biography of Bharo-Maimed Hand: A Tenth Century Bajracharya from Nepal', *Buddha Jayanti Smarika 2051 B.S.*, Lalitpur Oku Bahal, 2051 B.S.
- Gellner, David N.: 'The Newar Buddhist Monastery: An Anthropological and Historical Typology', in Neil Gutschow and Michael Allen (Ed.), *Heritage of the Kathmandu Valley: Proceedings of an International Conference in Lubeck*, June, 1985.
- Greenwold, Stephen: 'The Role of Priest in Newar Society', in James F. Fisher (ed.), *Himalayan Anthropology*, The Hague, Mounton, 1978.
- Greenwold, Stephen: 'Monkhood Versus Priesthood In Newar Buddhism', in Fuhrer Haimendorf (ed.), *Contribution to The Anthropology of Nepal*, Warminster, Aris and Philips, 1974.
- Kooij, Karel Rijik Van: 'The Iconography of The Buddhist Wood Carving', *Journal of Nepal Research Center*, Vol. I, 1997.
- 'Korean Zen Taking Root in The West', *Korean News Review*, Vol. 22, No. 14, April 3, 1993, Seoul.
- Levi, Sylvan, 'Le Nepal', *Kailas* Vol. 3, No.1, 1975 'Pashupati Vajragharko Narendra Devako Abhilekh', *Purnima,* Vol. 14, Year 4, No. 2, 2024 B.S.

- Locke, John K., 'Newar Buddhist Initiation Rites', *Contribution to Nepalese Studies* Vol. 2, No. 2, June 1975, CNAS.
- Shakya, Min Bahadur, 'Historical Analysis of Monasticism In Newar Buddhism', *Voice of History,* Vol. XI, No. 1, Kirtipur; 2000.
- Shakya, Min Bahadur: *Preservation of Sanskrit Buddhist MSS in the Kathmandu Valley: Its Importance and Future*, paper presented at Berkeley Buddhist Research Center California, 1998.
- Thapa, Shanker: 'Caste and Social Domination', *Ancient Nepal* No. 105, Kathmandu, Department of Archaeology, 1988.
- Thapa, Shanker: 'Textual History of Pancharaksya Sutra in Nepal', *Voice of History*, Vol. XV, No. 2, June 2000.
- Tuladhar, Sumon Kamal, 'Gwaye Da Tayegu: An Initial Ritual of the Samyaka Guthi' *Contribution to Nepalese Studies*, Vol. VII, No. 1 and 2, Dec. 1979 & Jan. 1980.
- Vajracharya, Indra Kumari, 'Nepalese Buddhist Monasteries in Aspects of Lakshmi Kalyan Varma Sanskarita Ratnakar Mahavihara of Patan', *Voice of History,* Vol. XI, No. 2, Kirtipur: 2057 B.S.

Journal Articles in Nepali

- Bhandari, Devi Prasad : 'Itihas Shiromani Babu Ram Acharyaley Tayar Garnubhayeko Nepalko Sankshipta Itihas', *Purnima,* Vol. 47, Year 12, No. 3, 2037 B.S.
- 'Hadigaonko Amshuvarmako Shilalekh', *Purnima,* Vol. 14, Year 4, No. 2, 2024 B.S.
- *Pasuka* Vol. 2, No. 11, N.S. 1118.
- 'Patan Yagbahalko Narendra Devako Abhilekh', *Purnima,* Vol. 14, Year 4, No. 2, 2024 B.S.
- Shakya, Milan : 'Nepali *Vihara* Ka Vishesta', *Paleswan,* Vol. IV, Lalitpur: Lotus Research Center, 1992.
- Vajracharya, Dhanavajra: 'Gum *Vihara*', *Madhuparka*, Year 4, No. 12, 2028.
- Vajracharya, Indra Kumari, 'Vajrayani Samajma Prachalit Thervadi Parampara' *Aananda Bhumi,* Vol. II, Year 29, Ananda Kuti Vihara, 2058 B.S.
- Vajracharya, Surya Man : 'Lalitpurko Baudha Vihara ra Bauddha, *Rajatjayanti Visheshanka,* (Silver Jubilee Souvenir), Lalitpur: Nepal Bauddha Vihara Sangha, 2057 B.S.

INDEX